What Is Form Criticism?

What Is Form Criticism?

by
Edgar V. McKnight

Fortress Press
Philadelphia

Library of Congress Catalog Card No. 71-81526

ISBN 0-8006-0180-7

Tenth Printing 1989

3912A89   Printed in the United States of America   1-180

Editor's Foreword

In New Testament scholarship insights, concerns, and positions may not change as much or as fast as they do in the natural sciences. But over the years they do change, and change a great deal, and they are changing with increasing rapidity. At an earlier period in the history of New Testament scholarship the Synoptic Gospels (Matthew, Mark, and Luke) were thought to be relatively uncomplicated documents which had been put together without careful planning and which told a rather straightforward story. Today the Synoptics are understood to be enormously intricate products containing subtle and ingenious literary patterns and highly developed theological interpretations. The three volumes in this series deal respectively with literary criticism, form criticism, and redaction criticism, and their purpose is to disclose something of the process whereby these disciplines have gained an enlarged understanding of the complex historical, literary, and theological factors which lie both behind and within the Synoptic Gospels. The volumes on form and redaction criticism will deal exclusively with the Synoptic Gospels, while the one on literary criticism will deal selectively with all the areas of the New Testament.

Literary criticism has traditionally concerned itself with such matters as the authorship of the various New Testament books, the possible composite nature of a given work, and the identity and extent of sources which may lie behind a certain document. More recently, however, biblical scholars have been paying attention to the criticism of fiction and poetry and to aesthetics and philosophy of language. Therefore the literary criticism of the New Testament has begun to reflect an interest in questions such as the relationship of content to form, the significance of structure or form for meaning, and the capacity of language to direct thought and to mold existence itself. The volume on literary criticism in this series will be sensitive to both the older and the newer aspects of the discipline.

The purpose of form criticism has been to get behind the sources which literary criticism might identify and to describe what was happening as the tradition about Jesus was handed on orally from person to person and from community to community. Form criticism has been especially concerned with the modifications which the life and thought of the church—both Jewish-Christian and gentile-Christian—have introduced into the tradition, and form critics have worked out criteria for distinguishing those strata in the Gospels which reflect the concerns of the church from the stratum that might be thought to go back to the historical Jesus. It has been shown that the church's vital life not only exerted a creative influence on the content of the tradition but also contributed formal characteristics, making it possible to classify much of the material in the Synoptics according to literary form. Form criticism has concerned itself largely with investigating the individual units—stories and sayings—in the Synoptic Gospels.

Redaction criticism is the most recent of the three disciplines to have become a self-conscious method of inquiry. It grew out of form criticism, and it presupposes and continues the procedures of the earlier discipline while extending and intensifying certain of them. The redaction critic investigates how smaller units—both simple and composite—from the oral tradition or from written sources were put together to form larger complexes, and he is especially interested in the formation of the Gospels as finished products. Redaction criticism is concerned with the interaction between an inherited tradition and a later interpretive point of view. Its goals are to understand why the items from the tradition were modified and connected as they were, to identify the theological motifs that were at work in composing a finished Gospel, and to elucidate the theological point of view which is expressed in and through the composition. Although redaction criticism has been most closely associated with the Gospels, there is no reason why it could not be used—and actually it is being used—to illuminate the relationship between tradition and interpretation in other New Testament books.

While each of the volumes in this series deals separately and focally with one of the methods of critical inquiry, each author is also aware of the other two methods. It has seemed wise to treat each of the three kinds of criticism separately for the purposes of definition, analysis, and clarification, but it should be quite clear that in actual practice the three are normally used together. They are not really separable. A New Testament scholar, in interpreting any book or shorter text or motif, would allow all three of the critical disciplines to contribute to his interpretation. An effort to demonstrate this inseparability might be made by taking a brief look at Mark 2:18–20:

> [18]Now John's disciples and the Pharisees were fasting; and people came and said to him, "Why do John's disciples and the disciples of the Pharisees fast, but your disciples do not fast?" [19]And Jesus said to them, "Can the wedding guests fast while the bridegroom is with them? As long as they have the bridegroom with them, they cannot fast. [20]The days will come, when the bridegroom is taken away from them, and then they will fast in that day.

This passage appears not only in Mark but is also a part of that substantial portion of Mark which serves as a source for Matthew and Luke (cf. Matt. 9:14–15; Luke 5:33–35) (literary criticism). Its outstanding formal features are a brief narrative (18) that provides a setting for a saying of Jesus (19a) which takes the form of a question and which is the real interest of the passage (form criticism). The question of fasting and the use of wedding imagery suggest a Jewish point of origin. At the same time we see a break with fasting and the attribution of joyful significance to the present—*today* is a wedding—rather than waiting for the future. These features suggest a modification of the Jewish setting. On the other hand, there is nothing, at least in 18–19a, which expresses the church's faith in Jesus' resurrection or the theological interpretation of Jesus' mission which grew out of that faith. This particular relationship to Judaism, on the one hand, and to distinctly Christian theology, on the other, gives to 18–19a a good claim to reflect the situation of the historical Jesus. However, 20 (and perhaps 19b) seems to grow out of a setting later than Jesus' own. Here we see the church basing the practice of fasting on Jesus' death (form criticism).

Our text is included in a collection of stories all of which present Jesus in conflict with the Jewish authorities (2:1–3:6) and which are concluded by the statement that Jesus' enemies took counsel how they might destroy him. Mark may have found the stories already collected, and a predecessor may also have added the concluding statement. But we do not know why the predecessor might have added it, while we can imagine why Mark would have. Jesus' death was very important for him, and it assumes a prominent place in his Gospel (redaction criticism).

If we might call the form of the Gospel as a whole a comedy which overcomes tragedy—the defeat of death by resurrection—we may then grasp the significance of our brief passage in that larger pattern. The slight allusion to Jesus' death anticipates the more direct hint in 3:6, which in turn prepares for the definite predictions of Jesus' death which begin at 8:31, predictions which are fulfilled in the final chapters of the Gospel. At the same time the resurrection is anticipated by the theme of the joyousness of today, which is further deepened by the note of irrepressible newness that appears in 2:21–22 (literary criticism). Our short text contributes to Mark's presentation of the reasons for Jesus' death—he challenged the established religious order—and Mark's understanding of the significance of Jesus' death and resurrection—a new, festal day has dawned offering to man freedom from compulsive ritualism (redaction and literary criticism).

It is hoped that the three volumes in this series will give to the interested layman new insight into how biblical criticism has illuminated the nature and meaning of the New Testament.

DAN O. VIA, JR.
University of Virginia

Contents

Preface

This book is intended to be a guided tour—a tour through the written Gospels back to the earthly Jesus. In the course of the tour you will see how the Gospel tradition passed from an oral stage in the earliest days of the church in Palestine to its written stage in our canonical Gospels. You will learn how the Gospels can be used historically to study the life and teachings of the earthly Jesus. Form criticism, the study of the tradition in its preliterary stage, is an important tool in the historical study, and this volume will introduce you to the discipline of form criticism.

I should like to express appreciation to my colleagues in the department of religion of Furman University for relieving me of some teaching duties in order to give me time to write this book. I am also grateful to the administration of Furman University for a grant to defray the expenses involved in the preparation of the manuscript.

EDGAR V. MCKNIGHT

I

The Origins of Form Criticism

A cursory glance at the Gospels could lead to the conclusion that it is a fairly easy task to write a full and accurate account of the life and teaching of Jesus. After all, there are four accounts in the New Testament. Two of the accounts (Matthew and John) bear the names of disciples who had been with Jesus and who (it is thought) doubtless gave complete, accurate reports of their experiences! Even the other two, according to tradition, are directly dependent upon earlier reports (Mark dependent upon Peter and Luke upon Paul).[1] The task is simply to arrange the materials of the Gospels into a unified story, a harmony. The Christian also brings to his reading of the Gospels a concept of Jesus from his religious tradition; the church's proclamation of Jesus Christ as Lord and the carefully developed doctrines of the church naturally influence the concept of Jesus gained in a reading of the Gospels.

The task (assuming the authorship of the Gospels by eyewitnesses and the authority of the church) is to organize the material of the Gospels into one harmonious account and to paraphrase, explain, and apply the materials for the benefit of the faithful. This was basically the method of the ancients. The title of one of the most important harmonies, that by the Reformed theologian Andrew Osiander in the sixteenth century, describes the method used: *Greek and Latin Gospel Harmony*

[1]All four of the Gospels were actually written anonymously. Later tradition, which may or may not have a basis in fact, has assigned names to each of the Gospels.

in Four Books, in Which the Gospel Story Is Combined According to the Four Evangelists in Such a Way that No Word of Any One of Them Is Omitted, No Foreign Word Added, the Order of None of Them Is Disturbed, and Nothing Is Displaced, in Which, However, the Whole Is Marked by Letters and Signs Which Permit One to See at a First Glance the Points Peculiar to Each Evangelist, Those Which He Has in Common with the Others, and with Which of Them.

The harmonizing of the Gospels and the interpretation of the resultant story of Jesus in prose, poetry, and drama continued into the eighteenth and nineteenth centuries—and continue among many Christians today—and the values of such a limited approach must not be ignored. Although there are values which derive from the precritical approach to the Gospels and to the life of Jesus, it is impossible for a student who is acquainted with the true nature of the Gospels and their witness to Jesus Christ to follow this method. The Gospels are not biographies of Jesus written for historical purposes by the original disciples of Jesus; rather, they are religious writings produced a generation after the earthly Jesus to serve the life and faith of the early church. However, the Gospels are based on earlier oral and written sources, and methods have been developed for moving through the tradition of the Gospels to the earthly Jesus.

This volume is concerned with form criticism, a discipline developed in the twentieth century and acknowledged by scholars to be a necessary and helpful method of dealing with the Gospel materials. Even an evangelical scholar who is the product of the American fundamentalism of the 1920's acknowledges that form criticism contains "certain valid elements" and "has thrown considerable light on the nature of the Gospels and the traditions they employ. Evangelical scholars should be willing to accept the light."[2] A representative of one of the larger popular Christian denominations in America says that form criticism is as much an improvement on source criticism as source criticism was an improvement over the traditional patterns of literalism. "It is difficult to overestimate

[2]George Eldon Ladd, *The New Testament and Criticism* (Grand Rapids: Eerdmans, 1967), pp. 148, 168–69.

the importance of this form-critical method."[3] W. D. Davies well says that "it should be recognized that all serious students of the New Testament today are to some extent Form Critics."[4] This chapter traces the developments in the study of Jesus and the Gospels which necessitated the development of form criticism and shows how the method first came to be applied to the New Testament.

THE NECESSITY FOR THE DISCIPLINE: DEVELOPMENTS IN SOURCE CRITICISM AND LIFE OF JESUS RESEARCH

The method of form criticism is a development of twentieth century scholarship, but its beginnings go back to the earliest critical studies of the Gospels and the life of Jesus. Simply stated, the eighteenth century witnessed the development of a critical approach to the life of Jesus, supplementing the traditional dogmatic approach of the church, and the nineteenth century saw a growth in the understanding of the nature and literary relationships of the only real sources for a study of Jesus—the canonical Gospels. The source criticism of the nineteenth century thus prepared the way for the form criticism of the twentieth century.

The first systematic critical study of Jesus was done by Hermann Samuel Reimarus (1694–1768), who stressed the claims of rational religion over against the dogma of the church and emphasized that a student must not approach Jesus from the perspective of the church's catechism but from the Jewish world of thought of Jesus' own day. Reimarus, however, did his work virtually in secret and did not publish any of his four-thousand-page, handwritten manuscript.[5] The work of Reimarus must be considered a "prologue" rather than a beginning of the critical study of the earthly Jesus, for the ideas of Reimarus did not directly influence the works which followed. Yet the forces at work in the life of Reimarus were at work in the

[3] S. A. Newman, "Review of *Rediscovering the Teaching of Jesus* by Norman Perrin," *The Quarterly Review*, 28(1968), 94.
[4] W. D. Davies, *Invitation to the New Testament* (Garden City: Doubleday, 1966), p. 97.
[5] G. E. Lessing issued seven "Fragments" of the work of Reimarus anonymously in a journal between 1774 and 1778. The largest of the "Fragments" (*Von dem Zwecke Jesu and seiner Jünger*) was published separately as a book in 1778.

life and thought of others in the eighteenth century who pioneered in the historical study of Jesus and who did influence the later developments in the study. These early rationalists continued to be influenced greatly by their relatively uncritical methodology and limited by the lack of an understanding of the nature and interrelationships of the Gospels. Yet, as a historian of the early studies of the life of Jesus says,

> We must not be unjust to these writers. What they aimed at was to bring Jesus near to their own time, and in so doing they became the pioneers of the historical studies of His life. The defects of their work in regard to aesthetic feeling and historical grasp are outweighed by the attractiveness of the purposeful, unprejudiced thinking which here awakens, stretches itself, and begins to move with freedom.[6]

In the eighteenth century, then, there was an increasing openness to reason in biblical study; in the nineteenth century attention was given to the relative merits of the first three Gospels (the Synoptic Gospels), on the one hand, and the Fourth Gospel (John), on the other, for a study of the life of Jesus, to the exact literary relationships between the first three Gospels, to the sources of the materials in these Gospels, and to related questions which bear on the use of these Gospels in the study of the life and teachings of Jesus.

When a presentation of the life of Jesus is attempted by connecting sections of the four Gospels into a "harmony," it becomes evident that the Gospel of John has a quite different chronological and geographical framework from that of the first three Gospels. In the account in the Synoptics Jesus makes only one journey to Jerusalem, but in John Jesus sets out three times from Galilee to Jerusalem (2:13; 5:1; 7:10). The final visit of Jesus to Jerusalem in the Synoptics continues for about a week, but in John it continues from a Feast of Tabernacles (7:2) to the Passover of Jesus' death, about half a year. The Synoptics imply that Jesus' entire ministry lasts no more than a year, but John's account demands a ministry of over two years. If an attempt is made to follow the account of the Fourth Gospel as well as the first three Gospels it becomes a

---

[6]Albert Schweitzer, *The Quest of the Historical Jesus: A Critical Study of its Progress from Reimarus to Wrede*, trans. W. Montgomery (2nd English ed.; London: Black, 1910), p. 29. (Hereafter cited as *Quest of the Historical Jesus.*)

matter of putting the material of the Synoptics into a Johannine framework. This was the basic procedure followed by the early writers on the life of Jesus. But such a use of the Gospel of John in the study of Jesus' life was questioned by D. F. Strauss in his *Life of Jesus* (1835–36).[7] He pointed out that the Johannine presentation of Jesus is clearly apologetic and dogmatic, and that it shows an even further development of tendencies seen already in the Synoptic Gospels. He asserted, therefore, that the nature of the Gospel of John makes it unsuitable as a source for the historical understanding of Jesus. This point was reinforced by later studies, especially by the work of F. C. Baur, and scholarly investigation began to focus on the Synoptic Gospels as sources.

That there are literary relationships between the Synoptic Gospels was noted long before the nineteenth century. A great number of narratives and discourses exist in more than one of the Gospels—frequently in all three—and the agreements extend beyond subject matter to the details of style and language. Compare the three accounts of the parable of the mustard seed:

Matt. 13:31–32	Mark 4:30–32	Luke 13:18–19
Another parable he put before them, saying, "The kingdom of heaven is like a grain of mustard seed which a man took and sowed in his field; it is the smallest of all seeds, but when it has grown it is the greatest of shrubs and becomes a tree, so that the birds of the air come and make nests in its branches."	And he said, "With what can we compare the kingdom of God, or what parable shall we use for it? It is like a grain of mustard seed, which, when sown upon the ground, is the smallest of all the seeds on earth; yet when it is sown it grows up and becomes the greatest of all shrubs, and puts forth large branches, so that the birds of the air can make nests in its shade."	He said therefore, "What is the kingdom of God like? And to what shall I compare it? It is like a grain of mustard seed which a man took and sowed in his garden; and it grew and became a tree, and the birds of the air made nests in its branches."

'David Friedrich Strauss, *The Life of Jesus*, trans. George Eliot (2 vols.; London: Chapman Bros., 1846).

5

Augustine (354–430), bishop of Hippo, was the first to con-
sider seriously the literary relationships among the Gospels.
He explained the relationships by the judgment that the Gospels originated in the sequence, Matthew, Mark, Luke, John,
and that the later Gospel writers had knowledge of the earlier
Gospels. Matthew is the earliest Gospel; Mark is an abridg-
ment of Matthew; and the later Gospels depend upon these
earlier ones. Although other theories were put forward to
explain the obvious literary relations of the Gospels, prior to
the nineteenth century the view of Augustine was the "ortho-
dox" position. Even Strauss held this position in his *Life of
Jesus.*

In the nineteenth century, however, a quite different solu-
tion to the Synoptic problem was reached by students of the
Gospels: Mark was the earliest of the canonical Gospels. The
authors of Matthew and Luke had Mark before them as they
wrote, and, therefore, the materials common to all three Gospels result from the use which Matthew and Luke made of
Mark. Matthew and Luke also used another source, now lost.
This non-Marcan source (called "Q," presumably an abbreviation of the German word for "source," *Quelle*) accounts for
the non-Marcan materials common to Matthew and Luke.
Finally, each used additional material which was not used
by the other.

Karl Lachmann, best known for his work on the Greek text
of the New Testament, seems to have been the first scholar
to support the priority of Mark from a careful study of the
facts. In 1835 he showed that, when Matthew and Luke used
material also found in Mark, the order of events in Matthew
and Luke corresponds closely, but that no such correspon-
dence in order exists when Matthew and Luke use material
which is not found in Mark. Lachmann, presupposing that
Matthew and Luke could not have used Mark, concluded that
all three Synoptic Gospels used an older written or oral source,
but that Mark followed the order of events in the older source
more accurately than did Matthew or Luke. Mark, therefore,
gives the tradition of the Gospels at an earlier stage than the
other Gospels.[8]

[8]Karl Lachmann, "De Ordine narrationum in evangeliis synopticis,"
Theologische Studien und Kritiken, 8 (1835), 570 ff.

Of course, even the scholarly world was slow in accepting the ideas of the priority of Mark and the use by Matthew and Luke of Mark and another source. This totally reversed the traditional view of Synoptic relationships. But by the end of the nineteenth century it had come to be looked upon as an assured result of the critical study of the Gospels. For the next quarter of a century, scholars were mainly occupied with additional documentary study—the attempt to trace and identify all of the various written documents beyond the Synoptic Gospels. Influential in the documentary quest was the presupposition that a history of Jesus would result. Scholars felt that, once all the documents had been isolated, their contents worked out, and their relation to the Synoptic Gospels determined, a scientific history of Jesus could be written.

A high point in the documentary study of the Gospels came in B. H. Streeter's *The Four Gospels: A Study of Origins* (1924).[9] He gathered up the results of the study of the Gospels in a systematic, comprehensive way. His most original contribution was the theory of the use of four *documents* in the origin of the Gospels. In addition to Mark and Q (the designation of the non-Marcan material common to Matthew and Luke), Streeter suggested that Matthew and Luke had documents peculiar to each which could be called M and L.

The supposition that the earliest documents, particularly Mark, carry us back directly to the earthly Jesus was shaken even before Streeter did his work. The studies of Wilhelm Wrede, Albert Schweitzer, Johannes Weiss, and Julius Wellhausen established the fact that Mark was not a simple, uncomplicated presentation of the life of the earthly Jesus. It cannot be presupposed that even the earliest documents carry us back directly to Jesus himself.

Wilhelm Wrede inaugurated this new turn in the interpretation of the Gospels by his work on the "Messianic Secret." He dealt most fully with the Gospel of Mark and indicated that in the Gospel of Mark there are not only historical but also, and more important, dogmatic ideas. The historical pattern of the events in Mark is given by Wrede: Jesus appeared as a teacher in Galilee surrounded by a circle of disciples with

[9]Burnett Hillman Streeter, *The Four Gospels: A Study of Origins* (rev. ed.; London: Macmillan, 1930).

whom he traveled and to whom he gave instruction. Besides teaching, Jesus is also pictured as performing miracles, especially the exorcism of demons. He associates with publicans and sinners and takes up an attitude of freedom in relation to the law. He encounters the opposition of the Pharisees and the Jewish authorities, who set traps for him and eventually, with the help of the Romans, bring about his death.[10]

But there is also a definite nonhistorical dogmatic content in Mark in which Jesus is presented in supernatural terms. He is the bearer of a special messianic office to which he is appointed by God. The real fact, according to Wrede, is that before the resurrection no one supposed that Jesus was the Messiah. But after the resurrection there was a tendency to interpret Jesus' ministry in messianic terms. The Gospel of Mark, therefore, attempts to give a messianic form to the non-messianic earthly life of Jesus. The tradition of the non-messianic character of Jesus' life was so strong, however, that the impulse to interpret Jesus messianically was not able to do away with the historical elements. Hence, the historical and dogmatic elements had to be harmonized.

Wrede claims that the historical and dogmatic conceptions are harmonized in the Gospel of Mark by means of an idea of intentional secrecy. Jesus is represented by the writer of Mark (so Wrede says) as keeping his Messiahship an almost complete secret while he is on earth. He does reveal himself as Messiah to his disciples; but he remains unintelligible even to them, and it is only with his resurrection that the true perception of what he is begins. Attention is called to significant data in the Gospel of Mark which support this theory. In the Gospel of Mark the demons who seek to make the identity of Jesus known are silenced (Mark 1:25, 34; 3:11–12). Secrecy is commanded after some of Jesus' mighty works have been accomplished (1:44; 5:43; 7:36; 8:26). After the confession of Peter and at the descent from the Mount of Transfiguration the disciples are charged to tell no one that Jesus is the Messiah (8:30; 9:9). Jesus withdraws from the multitudes; he embarks upon secret travels and moves around Galilee un-

[10]William Wrede, *Das Messiasgeheimnis in den Evangelien* (Göttingen: Vandenhoeck und Ruprecht, 1901; reissued, Vandenhoeck und Ruprecht, 1963), p. 130.

known (7:24; 9:30). He instructs the disciples privately concerning "the secret of the kingdom of God" and other subjects (4:10–12; 7:17–23; 8:31; 9:28–29; 31, 33–35; 10:33–34; 13:3–37).

Scholars following Wrede have not unanimously followed his theory of the "Messianic Secret" as a means of harmonizing the historical and theological in Mark, but they have reinforced his view that Mark was not merely a historical presentation of the earthly Jesus. Albert Schweitzer's work on the life of Jesus, published the same year that Wrede published his work, reinforced Wrede's view that Mark is not mere history.[11] Mark, indeed, is made up of a number of independent units and is not a closely connected historical narrative at all. Suggestive analogies are used to express this view:

> The material with which it has hitherto been usual to solder the sections [of Mark] together into a life of Jesus will not stand the temperature test. Exposed to the cold air of critical skepticism it cracks; when the furnace of eschatology is heated to a certain point the solderings melt. In both cases the sections all fall apart.
>
> Formerly it was possible to book through-tickets . . . which enabled those travelling in the interests of Life-of-Jesus construction to use express trains, thus avoiding the inconvenience of having to stop at every little station, change, and run the risk of missing their connexion. This ticket office is now closed. There is a station at the end of each section of the narrative, and the connexions are not guaranteed.[12]

The works of Johannes Weiss[13] and Julius Wellhausen[14] served to strengthen the view that Mark is not mere history and to call attention to the activity of the early Christian community in the formation of Mark.

By the early part of the twentieth century the critical study of the Synoptic Gospels had arrived at the following positions: (1) The "two document" hypothesis was accepted. Mark and Q served as sources for Matthew and Luke. (2) Both Mark and Q, as well as Matthew and Luke, were influenced by the

[11]Albert Schweitzer, *The Mystery of the Kingdom of God: The Secret of Jesus' Messiahship and Passion*, trans. Walter Lowrie (New York: Dodd, Mead, and Co., 1914).

[12]Schweitzer, *Quest of the Historical Jesus*, pp. 331–32.

[13]Johannes Weiss, *Das älteste Evangelium* (Göttingen: Vandenhoeck und Ruprecht, 1903).

[14]Julius Wellhausen, *Das Evangelium Marci* (Berlin: Reimer) was published in 1903, and in the next five years commentaries appeared on Matthew, Luke, and John.

9

theological views of the early church. (3) Mark and Q contained not only early authentic materials but also materials of a later date. Therefore, the discipline of source criticism did not bring scholars to pure historical sources which allowed them to arrive at an unbiased primitive view of the earthly Jesus. Some other tool was necessary! But what tool could be used to pry beyond Mark and Q into the preliterary stage of the Synoptic Gospels?

THE POSSIBILITY FOR THE DISCIPLINE:
GUNKEL'S STUDY
OF LEGENDS

A study of the early oral stages of a literature known to us only in a later written form sounds like an impossibility! But the truth is that studies had been undertaken which would enable scholars to pry back into the preliterary stages of the Synoptic Gospels. The scholar who made the greatest direct contribution by showing the actual possibility of form criticism was Hermann Gunkel, an Old Testament scholar. He applied form criticism to the first book of the Bible, Genesis. The first five books of the Old Testament (known collectively as the Pentateuch) parallel in many ways the Gospels of the New Testament. Although tradition attributes them to Moses (as tradition attributes the Gospels to the apostles), a careful study of the materials indicates that they assumed their present form over a long period of time and that a number of documents, no longer extant, were used in the composition of the books. Before the end of the nineteenth century, scholars had arrived at "assured results" concerning these sources. The documents, however, did not carry scholars back to the period of the events recounted in the books of the Pentateuch. Some tool besides source criticism was seen to be necessary to go behind the earliest documents. Hermann Gunkel was the Old Testament scholar who developed just that tool.

Gunkel acknowledged the results of source criticism, that Genesis (and the other books of the Pentateuch) grew out of previous documents which may be attributed to the Yahwist (J) of the ninth century B.C., the Elohist (E) of the first half of the eighth century, and the Priestly writer (P) between

500 and 444. The documents were combined and edited by later writers to form our present books: J and E were united near the time of the end of the kingdom of Judah (587); and this combined work, JE, was united with P about the time of Ezra (444). Before the documents were written, however, there were individual stories which originally existed in an oral form and which only later were placed in a structured collection. In order to study the early history of the stories they must be studied as individual units, not as they now stand in the Book of Genesis. Gunkel's view of the nature of the earliest documents assisted him in his work, for the earliest documents were not literary works composed by authors. The Yahwist and the Elohist were *collectors*, not authors; and although the Priestly writer may have been a genuine author responsible for a literary creation, he too used previous materials which can be isolated and studied as independent stories. Gunkel saw these originally oral stories as being developed and modified within the life of Israel over a long period of time. As some of the stories were carried into Israel from foreign countries and as all of the stories traveled into different parts of Israel, they were adapted to the existing life of the people. The stories also changed as they were transmitted from one age to a succeeding age. "When a new generation has come, when the outward conditions are changed or the thoughts of men have altered, whether it be in religion or ethical ideals or aesthetic taste, the popular legend cannot permanently remain the same. Slowly and hesitatingly, always at a certain distance behind, the legends follow the general changes in conditions, some more, others less."[15]

Gunkel classified the stories of Genesis in light of the purposes of the stories. He acknowledged that some legends are "historical" in that they reflect historical occurrences, they contain the remnant of a tradition of some actual event. But he emphasized that legends in general arose in Israel for the purpose of explaining something and he classified several different types of legends on the basis of what it is that they ex-

[15]Hermann Gunkel, *The Legends of Genesis: The Biblical Saga and History*, trans. W. H. Carruth (New York: Schocken, 1964), pp. 98–99. *The Legends of Genesis* is a translation of the introduction to Gunkel's *Genesis* (Göttingen: Vandenhoeck und Ruprecht, 1901).

11

plain: ethnological legends, etymological legends, ceremonial legends, and geological legends.

Ethnological legends are fictitious stories which were devised to explain the relations of tribes. The story of Jacob's deception, for example, explains how he obtained the better country.

Etymological legends resulted from the thought given by ancient Israel to the origin and meaning of the names of races, mountains, wells, sanctuaries, and cities. The explanation in the legend is not scientific but popular, based on the language as it stood. "It identifies the old name with a modern one which sounds more or less like it, and proceeds to tell a little story explaining why this particular word was uttered under these circumstances and was adopted as the name."[16] Jacob is interpreted as "heelholder" (*'āqēbh*), for example, because at birth he held his brother by the heel.

The important ceremonial legends seek to explain the existence of religious ceremonies which had come to play such an important part in Israel. What is the origin of the Sabbath, of circumcision? The real origin cannot be given, so the people tell a story to explain the sacred customs. The rite of circumcision, for example, is in memory of Moses, whose firstborn was circumcised as a redemption for Moses (Exod. 4:24–26).

Geological legends explain the origin of a locality. "Whence comes the Dead Sea with its dreadful desert? The region was cursed by God on account of the terrible sin of its inhabitants. Whence comes the pillar of salt with its resemblance to a woman? That is a woman, Lot's wife, turned into a pillar of salt as punishment for attempting to spy out the mystery of God (xix. 26)."[17] Of course, various motifs are frequently combined in one legend and some legends cannot readily be classified.

Gunkel felt that the history of the legend can be derived from a careful study of the legend itself because it shows the result of changes in time and place in itself. Slight additions, extensive additions, and in rare cases an entire story have been added to the tradition. Such additions may be recognized by the fact that they are out of place in an otherwise harmonious

---

[16]*Ibid.*, p. 28.
[17]*Ibid.*, p. 34.

story and by the fact that they are relatively unconcrete. Since the art of storytelling degenerated after the high point which gave the legends their initial form, later additions show more care for the thought than for the form of the story. Such later additions usually contain speeches and sometimes short narrative notes. The note that Jacob bought a field in Shechem (33:18–20) and that Deborah died and was buried at Bethel (35:8) are such narrative notes.

More important than the additions are the omissions which are intended to remove objectionable features. Gaps in the narrative give evidence of such omission. "Indeed, to those of a later time often so much had become objectionable or had lost its interest that some legends have become mere torsos." The case of the marriage with angels and the story of Reuben are such torsos. "In other cases only the names of the figures of the legend have come down to us without their legends."[18] The names of the patriarchs Nahor, Iscah, Milcah, Phichol, and Ahuzzath are illustrations. The legend of the giant Nimrod has been cut so that we have only the proverbial phrase, "like Nimrod, a mighty hunter before the Lord" (10:9). Some stories lost their context in transmission and were not correctly understood by later writers. The later narrators, for example, do not know why Noah's dove brought an olive leaf (8:11) or why Judah was afraid to give his youngest son to Tamar (38:11).

Hence there is spread over many legends something like a blue haze which veils the colors of the landscape: we often have a feeling that we indeed are still able to recall the moods of the ancient legends, but the last narrators had ceased to have a true appreciation of these moods. We must pursue all these observations, find the reasons that led to the transformations, and thus describe the inner history of the legends.[19]

THE EARLIEST WORK IN NEW TESTAMENT FORM CRITICISM

With the necessity for a study of the preliterary period of Gospel origins established by New Testament scholars and the possibility for preliterary study established by Gunkel in his research on Genesis, it was inevitable that the form critical

---

[18]*Ibid.*, p. 101.
[19]*Ibid.*, pp. 101–102.

approach would be applied to the Gospel tradition. Three scholars are credited with beginning this new effort in the study of the Gospels in the years 1919 through 1921. In 1919 came *Der Rahmen der Geschichte Jesu* [The Framework of the Story of Jesus] by Karl Ludwig Schmidt and *Die Formgeschichte des Evangeliums* (English translation: *From Tradition to Gospel,* 1935) by Martin Dibelius. These were followed in 1921 by Rudolf Bultmann's *Geschichte der synoptischen Tradition* (English translation: *History of the Synoptic Tradition,* 1963).

Karl Ludwig Schmidt was only twenty-eight years old when he published his book. It was his first book and established his reputation as a New Testament scholar. The title indicates the concern of the book—the framework within which the Gospel writers placed the life of Jesus. As was seen earlier, this was not a new concern. Earlier scholars such as D. F. Strauss had dealt with this. But Schmidt did a comprehensive study of the entire Gospel tradition and come to conclusions which both demanded and enabled New Testament scholars to pry back of the Gospels into the earlier oral period.

Schmidt accepted the conclusions of scholars as to the relations of the Synoptic Gospels—that Mark was the earliest of the Synoptic Gospels and that it was used by Matthew and Luke along with non-Marcan materials. But he along with some earlier scholars saw in addition that the Gospels—Mark included—are made up of short episodes which are linked together by a series of bridge passages which provide chronology, geography, and a movement of the life of Jesus from his early ministry to his arrest. The passion narrative is an exception, for it reached something like its present form at an early date and the individual units in the passion narrative have meaning *only* as they fit into place as parts of a larger whole. The passion narrative as a unit came into existence very early to answer the question asked in the early period of the church's activity, "How could Jesus have been brought to the cross by the people who were blessed by his signs and wonders?"[20]

By a careful study of the tradition Schmidt concluded that

---

[20]Karl Ludwig Schmidt, *Der Rahmen der Geschichte Jesu* (Berlin: Trowitzsch, 1919; reissued, Wissenschaftliche Buchgesellschaft, 1964), p. 305.

the Marcan framework itself was not original, that the Gospel writer provided the framework in the light of his own interests. His concluding paragraph points out that the lack of relationship between the units in Mark, the oldest Gospel, shows that the oldest tradition of Jesus consisted of an abundance of individual stories which have been united by early Christians with their different religious, apologetic, and missionary interests. "Only now and then, from considerations about the inner character of a story, can we fix these somewhat more precisely in respect to time and place. But as a whole there is no life of Jesus in the sense of an evolving biography, no chronological sketch of the story of Jesus, but only single stories, *pericopae,* which are put into a framework."[21] The work of the evangelist as seen in the completed Gospel is important for understanding the life and thought of the church of his day. But for the earlier history we are dependent upon the single episodes.

The episodes obviously came from the Christian believers among whom they circulated singly in oral form. They were preserved and transmitted because they met the needs of the church as a worshiping community.

If it is the case that the rise of the Christian faith can be understood only in terms of the development of Christian worship—a view which has won increasingly wide acceptance in recent years—it is clear that the rise of Christian literary activity must also be understood in relation to the experience of worship. In my opinion, the significance of the early Christian tradition of worship for the process of which the literature of the Gospels came into being cannot possibly be exaggerated.[22]

Schmidt carefully studied the entire Synoptic tradition from the perspective of the framework which the Gospel writers gave to the life of Jesus. He also gave some helpful suggestions as to the nature and origin of the individual units making up the Synoptic tradition. But Schmidt did not really utilize the tools of form criticism to pry back into the oral period of Gospel origins. This task was left for Martin Dibelius and Rudolf Bultmann.

Dibelius was the first to apply form criticism to the Synoptic tradition. Indeed the term "form criticism" [*Formge-*

[21]*Ibid.,* p. 317.
[22]*Ibid.,* p. 31.

schichte] came to be used in biblical studies because the title of his 1919 volume was *Die Formgeschichte des Evangeliums.* Dibelius's purpose was to explain by reconstruction and analysis "the origin of the tradition about Jesus, and thus to penetrate into a period previous to that in which our Gospels and their written sources were recorded" and "to make clear the intention and real interest of the earliest tradition."[23]

Bultmann's volume first appeared in 1921, two years after that of Dibelius, with the purpose of "discovering what the original units of the synoptics were, both sayings and stories, to try to establish what their historical setting was, whether they belonged to a primary or secondary tradition or whether they were the product of editorial activity."[24] Bultmann submitted the entire Synoptic tradition to a searching analysis; and, although Dibelius was the first of the two writers, Bultmann's name and method of analysis have been more closely associated with form criticism than has the name of Dibelius. Because of the significance of Dibelius and Bultmann in New Testament form criticism, the whole of the following chapter will deal with the method of these men.

[23]Martin Dibelius, *From Tradition to Gospel*, trans. Bertram Lee Woolf (New York: Scribner's, 1935), p. iii.
[24]Rudolf Bultmann, *History of the Synoptic Tradition*, trans. John Marsh (New York: Harper, 1963), pp. 2–3.

II

The Discipline Applied by Dibelius and Bultmann

Form criticism has not remained static. Because of its very nature it has changed as new insights have been gained into New Testament literature and history. Yet the modifications have been in line with the initial work of Dibelius and Bultmann; therefore knowledge and general acceptance of the work of these men is presupposed and necessary for understanding and using the discipline of form criticism.

PRESUPPOSITIONS

Form criticism moves from the existing text of the Synoptic Gospels to an earlier stage which does not now exist. In order to do this, certain things must be established or presupposed about the nature, origin, and transmission of the materials.

Source Criticism

The early form critics accept and build upon the conclusions of source criticism. The literary interdependence of the Gospels provides us with a profitable tool for form criticism. We can observe how Marcan and Q material is treated by Matthew and Luke, and we may assume that the same principles at work during the written period were operative on the traditional material even before it was given its form in Mark and Q. Source criticism, however, is merely the starting point for form criticism, for when form criticism is seen as the task of discovering the original units of the Synoptic tradition and of establishing the earlier history of the units, the written source of any particular unit is a matter of indifference.

17

Independent Units of Tradition

The "fundamental assumption," and in some sense the assumption which makes form criticism both necessary and possible, is that the tradition consists basically of individual sayings and narratives joined together in the Gospels by the work of the editors. The assumption of original individual units does not mean that there were no collections before the work of the Gospel writers. K. L. Schmidt had concluded that such earlier collections did in fact exist, and Dibelius and Bultmann acknowledge that small groups of materials were formed in the oral period. Dibelius says, "That narratives were united even in the old tradition, is seen most clearly in the interweaving of the story of Jairus with the healing of the woman with the issue. The union is so close here, that we cannot regard it as originating in the evangelist as editor."[1] Bultmann stresses, however, that "there is a natural limit to such groupings in the oral period, even if it cannot be precisely defined, a limit which can be exceeded for the first time in the written tradition."[2]

The Passion Narrative

One body of material is seen as an exception to the rule that there were no connected narratives of the life of Jesus in the earliest period. This exception is the Passion narrative. The earliest Passion story, however, is not the Marcan story. Both Dibelius and Bultmann hold that the Marcan story is the end result of a very early process of transmission of tradition and that even in the earliest Passion story that we can reconstruct we do not have pure history. We do have in the Passion narrative of the Synoptics an early composition of a *connected narrative,* a narrative which gives events in a larger context. This is an important exception to the general history of the Synoptic tradition.

The Tradition and the Church

The tradition served the needs and purposes of the church. This assumption is vital for Dibelius since he follows a constructive method and reconstructs the history of the Synoptic tradition from a study of the early Christian community. Even

[1]Dibelius, *From Tradition to Gospel,* p. 219.
[2]Bultmann, *History of the Synoptic Tradition,* p. 322.

though Bultmann follows an analytical method which begins with the text instead of the church, he admits that he cannot "dispense with a provisional picture of the primitive community and its history, which has to be turned into a clear and articulated picture in the course of my inquiries."[3]

The assumption that the tradition is church-oriented makes very important the specific view of the primitive community and its history which Dibelius and Bultmann hold. Dibelius sees the Christian movement as originating with the Aramaic-speaking Palestinian circle of Jesus, of course. Then comes a pre-Pauline Hellenistic Christianity in close proximity to Judaism. These pre-Pauline Christian churches were in Greek-speaking regions such as Antioch and Damascus and grew out of Jewish churches without making a logical break with Judaism. Still later comes the Pauline church which is much less closely related to Judaism.

Dibelius declares that the Synoptic tradition did not acquire its form in the Aramaic-speaking Palestinian church or in the later Pauline church. The tradition acquired its form in the pre-Pauline Hellenistic churches closely associated with Judaism. These churches emphasized that the faith and hopes of Judaism reached completion with the coming of the Messiah, Jesus Christ.[4] This Christianity was especially interested in the traditions of the life of Jesus from the perspective that the long-expected salvation had now come to pass in the events of Jesus among the Jewish people. The churches were not interested in the tradition for literary and historical purposes. They were interested in a tradition to be passed on to missionaries, preachers, and teachers. This concern for preaching led to the cultivation and formation of the tradition. Such concern might require that "the material should be shaped and directed for the purposes which it should serve, i.e. definitely sharpened, obscure points made clear, the material placed in closer connection with the subject of the sermon, and the actual interests of the life of the Church introduced."[5]

Bultmann cannot dispense with a provisional picture of the primitive community and its history in his analysis of the Syn-

[3]Ibid., p. 5.
[4]Dibelius, From Tradition to Gospel, p. 30.
[5]Ibid., p. 31.

19

optic tradition. But his approach does not demand as detailed a picture of the church as does the approach of Dibelius. Hence Bultmann is satisfied to divide early Christianity into two basic phases: Palestinian Christianity and Hellenistic Christianity.

Classification of Form

Dibelius and Bultmann assume that the materials can be classified as to form and that the form enables the students to reconstruct the history of the tradition. Dibelius says that a careful critical reading of the Gospels shows that the Gospel writers took over units of material which already possessed a form of their own. Dibelius is not speaking of aesthetic standards created by a gifted individual when he speaks of the "form" of a tradition. He is speaking of the "style" of a unit— a style or form that has been created by its use among early Christians. The specific use to which a unit is put determines its form, and in the case of the early church the forms developed out of primitive Christian life itself. The units, therefore, have a form which is related to their place in the life of the church. "We are concerned . . . not with things remembered complete in themselves, though without form, and thus passed on, but, from the very beginning, with recollections full of emotional power to bring about repentance and to gain believers. Thus the things which were remembered automatically took on a definite form, for it is only when such matters have received a form that they are able to bring about repentance and gain converts."[6] Form criticism, then, must inquire into the life and worship of early Christianity and ask what categories are possible or probable in this community of unliterary people.

Bultmann is in complete accord with this assumption. "The proper understanding of form-criticism rests upon the judgment that the literature . . . springs out of quite definite conditions and wants of life from which grows up a quite definite style and quite specific forms and categories."[7] Every literary category then will have its own "life situation" [*Sitz im Leben*] which is a typical situation in the life of the early Christian community.

[6] *Ibid.*, pp. 13–14.
[7] Bultmann, *History of the Synoptic Tradition*, p. 4.

LITERARY FORMS AND THEIR *SITZ IM LEBEN*

Both Dibelius and Bultmann, following the example of a form critical study of the Old Testament, find a variety of forms in the Synoptic Gospels.

The Forms of Dibelius

The main concern of Dibelius is with the narrative material of the Gospels, and he finds three major categories of narrative material in addition to the Passion narrative. The Passion story came first. It was told relatively early as a connected story. Then paradigms developed. These were short stories which told of isolated events in the life of Jesus and which were suitable for sermons. When pleasure in the narrative for its own sake arose, the technique of the tale [*Novelle*] developed. Also, legendary narratives growing out of personal interest in the individuals involved with Jesus developed and joined themselves to the periphery of the tradition.

Paradigm. The sermons of the early Christians did not contain simply the bare message of the gospel "but rather the message as explained, illustrated and supported with references and otherwise developed."[8] The narratives of the deeds of Jesus were introduced as examples to illustrate and support the message. These *examples* constitute the oldest Christian narrative style, and hence Dibelius suggests the name "paradigm" for this category of narrative.

The tribute money (Mark 12:13–17) is a pure paradigm:

And they sent to him some of the Pharisees and some of the Herodians, to entrap him in his talk. And they came and said to him, "Teacher, we know that you are true, and care for no man; for you do not regard the position of men, but truly teach the way of God. Is it lawful to pay taxes to Caesar, or not? Should we pay them, or should we not?" But knowing their hypocrisy, he said to them, "Why put me to the test? Bring me a coin, and let me look at it." And they brought one. And he said to them, "Whose likeness and inscription is this?" They said to him, "Caesar's." Jesus said to them, "Render to Caesar the things that are Caesar's, and to God the things that are God's." And they were amazed at him.

The following units (with parallels in other Gospels at times) are also judged to be pure paradigms: Mark 2:1–12, 18–22,

---

'Dibelius, *From Tradition to Gospel,* p. 25.

23–28; 3:1–5, 20–30, 31–35; 10:13–16; 12:13–17; 14:3–9. Other less pure paradigms include: Mark 1:23–27; 2:13–17; 6:1–6; 10:17–22, 35–40, 46–52; 11:15–19; 12:18–23; Luke 9:51–56; 14:1–6.

From a study of the paradigms themselves Dibelius finds five essential characteristics: (1) independence from the literary context, (2) brevity and simplicity for use as examples in a sermon, (3) religious rather than artistic coloring and style, (4) didactic style often causing the words of Jesus to stand out clearly, and (5) an ending in a thought useful for preaching, a word or act of Jesus or the reaction of the onlookers.

Tales. The tales in the Gospels are stories of Jesus' miracles which originate in their present form not with preachers but with storytellers and teachers who related the stories from the life of Jesus "broadly, with colour, and not without art."[9] Indeed, "*literary style in reporting miracles,* a feature which we missed on the whole from Paradigms, . . . appears in the Tales with a certain regularity."[10] The style of the tales compares with the style of similar stories from ancient to modern times: First comes the history of the illness, then the technique of the miracle, and finally the success of the miraculous act. "Tales belong to a higher grade of literature than paradigms."[11]

The first tale in Mark is the healing of a leper (Mark 1:40–45). (The miracle recounted in 1:23–27 is a paradigm, not a tale.)

And a leper came to him beseeching him, and kneeling said to him, "If you will, you can make me clean." Moved with pity, he stretched out his hand and touched him, and said to him, "I will; be clean." And immediately the leprosy left him, and he was made clean. And he sternly charged him, and sent him away at once, and said to him, "See that you say nothing to any one; but go, show yourself to the priest, and offer for your cleansing what Moses commanded, for a proof to the people." But he went out and began to talk freely about it, and to spread the news, so that Jesus could no longer openly enter a town, but was out in the country; and people came to him from every quarter.

[9]*Ibid.*, p. 70.
[10]*Ibid.*, p. 82.
[11]*Ibid.*, p. 103.

Other Synoptic tales are found in the following units: Mark 4:35–41; 5:1–20, 21–43; 6:35–44, 45–52; 7:32–37; 8:22–26; 9:14–29; Luke 7:11–16.

The tales are similar to paradigms in that they are individual stories complete in themselves.[12] But in almost every other way they differ. The tales are much longer than paradigms, and they contain a greater breadth of description due to story-tellers and teachers "who understand their art and who love to exercise it."[13] There is also a *"lack of devotional motives and the gradual retreat of any words of Jesus of general value"*[14] in the tales. The conclusions do not contain material useful for preaching such as we find in paradigms. Clearly the tales do not play a part in the sermon as do the paradigms. They exist for the pleasure of the narrative itself.

Tales originated, according to Dibelius, in three ways: by extending paradigms, by introducing foreign motifs, or by borrowing foreign material. The process of extending paradigms was somewhat automatic when the paradigms were set free from their context in a sermon. The storytellers and teachers, "men who were accustomed to narrate according to the plan of the usual miracle-stories or in the style of current anecdotes,"[15] introduced a richer miracle content into the paradigms and they employed all the usual narrative elements to make the tales lively. Also, brief paradigmatic narratives were extended by employing motifs perhaps strange to the original paradigm. For example, Dibelius feels that the story of Jesus walking on the water (Mark 6:45–52 and parallel passage, Matt. 14:22–33) may have resulted from the intro-duction of an epiphany motif (manifestation of the divine on earth) into a primitive narrative of Jesus intervening helpfully in a difficulty caused by winds and waves. At times non-Chris-tian stories were simply taken over as wholes.

[12]The account of the healing of the woman with the issue and the raising from the dead in the house of Jairus is an exception. "The at-tempt to separate them would completely destroy the structure of the main, together with the subsidiary narrative." *Ibid.*, p. 72.

[13]*Ibid.*, p. 76.
[14]*Ibid.*, p. 79.
[15]*Ibid.*, p. 99.

Legends. Legends, "religious narratives of a saintly man in whose works and fate interest is taken,"[16] arose in the church to satisfy a double desire: the desire to know something of the human virtues and lot of the holy men and women in the story of Jesus and the desire which gradually developed to know Jesus himself in this way. The story of Jesus when he is twelve years old (Luke 2:41–49) is the story of Jesus which shows most clearly the qualities of legend.

It is natural to think of legend as entirely unhistorical, and Dibelius acknowledges that the religious interests of the narrator may "lead to an unhistorical accentuation of the miraculous, to a glorifying of the hero and to a transfiguration of his life."[17] Yet, Dibelius stresses that it would be wrong to deny historical content to every legend in the Synoptic Gospels. "A narrator of legends is certainly not interested in historical confirmation, nor does he offer any opposition to increasing the material by analogies. But how much historical tradition he hands on in a legend depends on the character of his tradition only."[18]

Myth. Dibelius is convinced that the story of Jesus is not of mythological origin; the paradigms, the oldest witness of the process of formation of the tradition, do not tell of a mythological hero. A Christ mythology, evident in the letters of Paul, did arise late in the process of the tradition's formation.

Dibelius judges that only to the smallest extent is the Synoptic tradition of a mythological character. The only narratives which describe a mythological event, "a many-sided interaction between mythological but not human persons,"[19] are the records of the baptismal miracle (Mark 1:9–11 and parallel passages), the temptation of Jesus (Mark 1:12–13 and parallel passages), and the transfiguration (Mark 9:2–8 and parallel passages).

Sayings. Although Dibelius emphasizes the narrative material of the Synoptic Gospels, he does deal with the sayings

[16]*Ibid.*, p. 104.
[17]*Ibid.*, p. 108.
[18]*Ibid.*, p. 109.
[19]*Ibid.*, p. 271.

of Jesus. He finds preaching, especially catechetical instruction, as the place of formulation of such teachings, but he presupposes a law different from the law concerning narrative material to be at work in the sayings of Jesus. Just as the Jews of Jesus' day took the rules of life and worship more seriously than they took historical and theological tradition, so the Christians treated the sayings of Jesus more seriously than the narratives. The sayings of Jesus were important, for they dealt with Christian life and worship, and, when the early Christian teachers transmitted the early exhortation, the words of Jesus were naturally included. Dibelius reminds us in this connection that "all the sayings of Christian exhortation were regarded as inspired by the Spirit or by the Lord. Thus all of them appeared as exhortations 'in the Lord', if not as exhortations of the Lord."[20]

As the sayings of Jesus were transmitted, however, some modification took place. The tradition emphasized and strengthened the hortatory character of the words of Jesus and thereby altered the meaning and emphasis of words which were not originally hortatory. There was also a tendency to include christological sayings so as "to obtain from the words of Jesus not only solutions of problems or rules for one's own life, but also to derive from them some indications about the nature of the Person who had uttered them."[21]

The Forms of Bultmann

Bultmann does a detailed analysis of all the Synoptic material within the two general divisions of the discourses of Jesus and the narrative material. The discourses of Jesus are divided into two main groups: apophthegms and dominical sayings; but Bultmann also gives a separate treatment of "I sayings" and parables although by content they belong to the dominical sayings. The narrative materials are also divided into two major groups: miracle stories and historical narratives and legends.

Apophthegms. Bultmann's category "apophthegms" is basically the same as Dibelius's "paradigms." It applies to short

[20] *Ibid.*, p. 241.
[21] *Ibid.*, p. 246.

sayings of Jesus set in a brief context. But Bultmann does not agree that the form arose in preaching in every case. Because of this he uses the term "apophthegm" instead of "paradigm" for it is a category from Greek literature denoting merely a short, pithy, and instructive saying which does not prejudge the matter of origin. Bultmann sees three different types of apophthegms characterized by the different settings or causes for the sayings. Controversy dialogues are occasioned by conflict over such matters as Jesus' healings or the conduct of Jesus and the disciples; scholastic dialogues arise through questions asked by opponents; biographical apophthegms are in the *form* of historical reports.

The Sabbath healing of the man with the withered hand in Mark 3:1–6 is an example of a *controversy dialogue*. Bultmann sees the controversy dialogues as literary devices arising in the discussions which the church had with its opponents and within itself on questions of law.

The question concerning the chief commandment in Mark 12:28–34 is a *scholastic dialogue*. There is a close relationship between the scholastic dialogue and the controversy dialogue. The essential difference between them, as the title indicates, is that in the scholastic dialogue a controversy is not the starting point, but for the most part the starting point is a question asked the Master by someone seeking knowledge.

The account in Luke 9:57–62 is a *biographical apophthegm*. Biographical apophthegms are so named because the apophthegm purports to contain information about Jesus. The specific starting point of the biographical apophthegm, although not of the controversy and scholastic dialogue, is the sermon. "The biographical apophthegms are best thought of as edifying paradigms for sermons. They help to present the Master as a living contemporary, and to comfort and admonish the Church in her hope."[22]

In Bultmann's opinion all three types of apophthegms are "ideal" constructions of the church. They are not historical reports. It is true that Jesus engaged in disputations and was asked questions about the way to life, the greatest commandment, and other matters. It is also true that the apophthegms could easily contain a historical reminiscence and that the

[22]Bultmann, *History of the Synoptic Tradition*, p. 61.

decisive saying of a dialogue may go back to Jesus himself. But the apophthegms as they stand are church constructions—Palestinian church constructions as may be seen by comparison with similar rabbinic stories. Hence most of the apophthegms were developed early in the life of the church.

Bultmann agrees with Dibelius that the apophthegm began to develop novel-like tendencies through an interest in history or in storytelling. "As soon as the apophthegm is affected by an interest in history or developed story telling we meet with more precise statements."[23] The questioners in the apophthegm, for example, are described specifically. They are characterized as opponents of Jesus or perhaps even as disciples, whereas they were originally unspecified individuals for the most part.

Dominical Sayings. The sayings of Jesus are divided by Bultmann into three main groups chiefly according to their actual content, although formal differences are also involved. The three groups are: proverbs, prophetic and apocalyptic sayings, and laws and community regulations.

The *proverb* shows Jesus as the teacher of wisdom comparable with teachers of wisdom in Israel, Judaism, and throughout the Orient. Three basic "constitutive" forms are used for the proverbs, forms conditioned by the sayings themselves. These forms exist in all proverbial literature, not only in the proverbial sayings in the Synoptic Gospels. The proverb in a *declarative form* sets forth a principle or a declaration concerning material things or persons. Examples from the Synoptic tradition include: "For out of the abundance of the heart the mouth speaks" (Matt. 12:34); "Let the day's own trouble be sufficient for the day" (Matt. 6:34); "The laborer deserves his wages" (Luke 10:7); and "Many are called, but few are chosen" (Matt. 22:14). Exhortations are placed in an *imperative form:* "Physician, heal yourself" (Luke 4:23); "Leave the dead to bury their own dead" (Matt. 8:22). Proverbs also exist in the *form of questions:* "And which of you by being anxious can add one cubit to his span of life?" (Matt. 6:27); "Can the wedding guests fast while the bridegroom is with them?" (Mark 2:19).

Ibid., p. 67.

Bultmann shows that there were developments in the proverbs even after they were written down, and that it is impossible to evade the question whether all proverbs go back to the earthly Jesus. The question is especially difficult when it is observed that Synoptic proverbs have parallels in Jewish wisdom literature. (Compare Luke 14:7–12 with Proverbs 25: 6–7, for example.) In regard to the genuineness of the proverbs, Bultmann sees several possibilities: that Jesus himself coined some of the proverbs which the Synoptics attribute to him, that Jesus occasionally made use of popular proverbs of his time, and that the primitive church placed in Jesus' mouth many wisdom sayings that were really derived from the storehouse of Jewish proverbial lore. Bultmann's judgment is that the wisdom sayings are "least guaranteed to be authentic words of Jesus; and they are likewise the least characteristic and significant for historical interpretation."[24]

Prophetic and apocalyptic sayings are those sayings in which Jesus "proclaimed the arrival of the Reign of God and preached the call to repentance, promising salvation for those who were prepared and threatening woes upon the unrepentant."[25] To this category belong sayings like: "The time is fulfilled, and the kingdom of God is at hand; repent, and believe in the gospel" (Mark 1:15); "Blessed are the eyes which see what you see! For I tell you that many prophets and kinds desired to see what you see, and did not see it, and to hear what you hear, and did not hear it" (Luke 10:23–34); "Blessed are you poor, for yours is the kingdom of God. Blessed are you that hunger now, for you shall be satisfied. Blessed are you that weep now, for you shall laugh" (Luke 6:20–21) are clearly in this category of sayings.

Bultmann sees proof in the little apocalypse of Mark 13:5–27 that Jewish material has been ascribed to Jesus by the church, and he asks to what extent the rest of the material must be similarly judged. In some sayings the immediacy of eschatological consciousness is so different from Jewish tradition that Jesus himself must have been the origin. (Luke 10:23–24;

[24]Rudolf Bultmann, "The Study of the Synoptic Gospels," *Form Criticism*, ed. and trans. Frederick C. Grant (New York: Harper, 1962), p. 55.
[25]*Ibid.*, p. 56.

Matt. 11:5–6; Luke 11:31–32; and Luke 12:54–56.) But there are other passages which contain nothing specifically characteristic of Jesus and where it is most likely that there was a Jewish origin (Matt. 24:37–41, 43–44, 45–51; Matt. 24:10–12; Luke 6:24–36; Luke 6:20–21.) Not all sayings which are judged unlikely to have originated in Judaism come from Jesus, for the early church formulated some passages. Some of the prophetic sayings were originally the work of early Christian prophets which were later attributed to the earthly Jesus. Such a church origin is more likely the more there is a relationship of the saying to the person of Jesus or to the lot and interest of the church. Bultmann asserts that "one may with perfect right recognize among them authentic words of Jesus; and though the Christian community itself produced many a prophetic saying, as may be clearly shown, it must nevertheless be recognized that, according to the testimony of the earliest Christians themselves, they owed their eschatological enthusiasm to the prophetic appearance of Jesus."[26]

The third group of sayings is made up of statements regarding *the law and Jewish piety* and *regulations of the early community*. Examples are: "There is nothing outside a man which by going into him can defile him; but the things which come out of a man are what defile him" (Mark 7:15); "Is it lawful on the Sabbath to do good or to do harm, to save life or to kill?" (Mark 3:4); and "If your brother sins against you, go and tell him his fault, between you and him alone. If he listens to you, you have gained your brother. But if he does not listen, take one or two others along with you, that every word may be confirmed by the evidence of two or three witnesses. If he refuses to listen to them, tell it to the church; and if he refuses to listen even to the church, let him be to you as a Gentile and a tax collector" (Matt. 18:15–17).

Bultmann declares that the history of the sayings can be seen "with desirable clarity" in the legal material. He indicates that the church possessed a stock of genuine sayings of Jesus. Especially important and genuine are the brief conflict sayings which express Jesus' attitude to Jewish piety (Mark 7:15; 3:4; Matt. 23:16–19, 23–24, 25–26). Concerning these

Ibid., pp. 56–57.

Bultmann says that "this is the first time that we have the right to talk of sayings of Jesus, both as to form and content."[27] The tradition gathered these genuine sayings, "gave them a new form, enlarged them by additions and developed them further; it collected other (Jewish) sayings, and fitted them by adaptation for reception into the treasury of Christian instruction, and produced new sayings from its consciousness of a new possession, sayings which they ingenuously put into the mouth of Jesus."[28] Bultmann especially attributes to the church the Old Testament citations which are frequently found in combination with debating sayings, the sayings which contain rules for the discipline of the community and for its mission, and the sayings in which the church expressed its faith in Jesus, his work, his destiny, and his person.

The *I sayings* are those sayings attributed to Jesus in which he speaks of himself, his work, and his destiny. "Think not that I have come to abolish the law and the prophets; I have come not to abolish them but to fulfil them" (Matt. 5:17), and "For the Son of man also came not to be served but to serve, and to give his life as a ransom for many" (Mark 10:45) illustrate the "I sayings." Bultmann admits that it is impossible to prove that Jesus could not have spoken in the first person about himself. But he brings such serious considerations against so many of these sayings that "one can have but little confidence even in regard to those which do not come under positive suspicion."[29] The sayings as a whole express the retrospective point of view of the church. Although some come from the Palestinian church (Matthew 5:17, for example, points to the legal debates of the early church and Matthew 15:24 points to discussions about the Gentile mission), the "I sayings" were predominantly the work of the Hellenistic churches.

The *parable* is a concise and simple story which is much like a popular story in its concrete language, its use of dialectical language and soliloquy, and its repetition. It is a story told to call forth judgment on the part of the hearer; a judgment is made regarding the story of everyday human affairs and

---

[27]Bultmann, *History of the Synoptic Tradition*, p. 147.
[28]*Ibid.*, pp. 145–46.
[29]*Ibid.*, p. 155.

relations, then the judgment is applied in the realm of the spiritual life.[30]

Jesus, of course, spoke in parables, but the church transmitted the parables and used them for its own purpose. It is clear that here and there the form has been changed and applications added to the parables to make them more relevant to the later church. Such alterations are even seen in Matthew's and Luke's use of their written sources. But Bultmann sees more radical alteration by the church. The parables have been placed into particular contexts and given introductions which affect the *meaning* of the stories. At times the church placed a new parable alongside an older independent story, the new parable being built along the same general lines and giving either the same teaching as the old parable or a modification of the original teaching. The church also enlarged parables by providing allegorical additions and explanations. Parables from the Jewish tradition were also used to augment the store of parables of Jesus.

The history of the parables in the tradition makes it clear that the original meaning of many of the parables of Jesus has become irrecoverable and that some of the parabolic material does not go back to Jesus but to the church. Bultmann concludes with a rule which enables us to discover genuine parables of Jesus. "We can only count on possessing a genuine similitude of Jesus where, on the one hand, expression is given to the contrast between Jewish morality and piety and the distinctive eschatological temper which characterized the preaching of Jesus; and where on the other hand we find no specifically Christian features."[31]

Miracle Stories. Bultmann divides the narrative material of the Synoptic Gospels into two main groups: miracle stories and historical narratives and legends. He means by "miracle stories" what Dibelius means by "tales," namely, stories of

---

[30]Bultmann finds different figurative forms ranging from simple comparisons and metaphors to similes [*Gleichnisse*], parables [*Parabeln*], and exemplary stories [*Beispielerzählungen*]. Distinctions are not always easy to observe, and all of the parables have in common the element of comparison.

[31]Bultmann, *History of the Synoptic Tradition,* p. 205.

healings and nature miracles in which the miracle constitutes the main theme and is described with considerable detail. Miracles occur among the apophthegms, but there the
miracle is subordinated to the point of the apophthegm.

Bultmann compares the Synoptic miracle stories with the
miracle stories of Jewish and Hellenistic origin and discovers
that the Gospel stories have exactly the same style as the
Hellenistic miracle stories. The condition of the sick person is
described, the healing is recounted, then the consequences of
the miracle are unfolded.

Bultmann asks at what stage the tradition was enriched by
the addition of miracle stories and concludes that a Palestinian
origin is probable for several miracle stories. "Judging Mk.
4:35–41 (Stilling of the Storm) by its content, a *Palestinian*
origin seems probable if the Jewish parallels are taken into
consideration. The same holds true for Mk. 6:34–44 or 8:1–9
(Feeding Stories). The healing of the leper (Mk. 1:40–45)
will also have come from the Palestinian Church." But, "for
the rest, the *Hellenistic* origin of the miracle stories is overwhelmingly the more probable."[32] The similarity between the
miracle stories in the Synoptic Gospels and those in Hellenistic
literature forces the conclusion that miracle stories by and
large do not belong to the oldest strata of tradition.

Historical Stories and Legends. Legends, in Bultmann's
definition, are religious and edifying narratives which are not
properly miracle stories, although they may include something
miraculous, and are not basically historical, although they may
be based on historical happenings. Bultmann treats historical
stories and legends together because he sees no possibility of
separating the two. He acknowledges that some passages are
purely legendary. An example is the narrative of the temptation of Jesus (Mark 1:12–13), which probably belongs to the
type of the "temptations of the holy men" like Buddha, Zarathustra, and later Christian saints who are tested by evil and
who emerge victorious. But even the stories with a historical
basis, in the view of Bultmann, "are so much dominated by
the legends that they can only be treated along with them."[33]

[32]*Ibid.*, p. 240.
[33]*Ibid.*, p. 245.

The historicity of Jesus' baptism by John, for example, is not to be disputed, but as the story is told in the Synoptic Gospels (Mark 1:9-11) it must be classified as a legend. Its purpose is not historical but religious and edifying. It tells of Jesus' consecration as Messiah and is a faith legend. (When the context is the faith or worship of the community, the result is a faith or cult legend; when the context is the life of some religious hero, the result is a biographical legend.)

Bultmann observes that the legendary motifs in the narratives are of diverse origin. Some materials show the influence of the Old Testament and Judaism, others show Hellenistic elements, still others have motifs which have grown up within the Christian tradition itself. The place at which the material came into the life of the church varies: Palestinian, Jewish Hellenistic, and purely Hellenistic. Regardless of the ultimate origin and time of utilization by the church, the materials were used to meet the needs of Christian faith and life.

FORM CRITICISM AND THE LIFE OF JESUS

The postulates of Dibelius and Bultmann, reinforced by their analysis of the Synoptic tradition, greatly affect their approach to the life of Jesus. The nature of the only real sources for the life of Jesus—the Synoptic Gospels—makes a biography impossible. The community which was most influential in the formation of the tradition was not concerned with a biography as such and did not transmit a connected, chronological, geographical outline of developments in the life of Jesus. It transmitted individual sayings and narratives, with the single exception of the passion narrative. Moreover, according to Dibelius and Bultmann, the individual units do not go back to Jesus. The church formulated them for its purposes! We do not delete "additions" here and there and get back to a primitive form from Jesus' day; we get back to the form which originated in the church. Yet, both Dibelius and Bultmann wrote books on Jesus, and it is instructive for those who wish to understand and use form criticism that these two men can begin with similar presuppositions regarding the formation of the tradition and yet arrive at diverse positions as to how the tradition can be used in a life of Jesus.

Dibelius and the Life of Jesus

Martin Dibelius published a book on Jesus in 1939[34] which was written on the basis of his earlier work in form criticism. Dibelius saw that a distinction was to be made between the historical reliability of various units of the tradition on the basis of the *form* of the units. The passion story is unique in the tradition and the general outline of the passion story is viewed by Dibelius as trustworthy.

Paradigms are the most historical of the three forms of narrative material because, like the passion narrative, they arose earliest among the eyewitnesses who could control and correct the tradition. Their place in the life of the church also assures their relative trustworthiness, for they arose in connection with preaching, and "the nearer a narrative stands to the sermon the less is it questionable, or likely to have been changed by romantic, legendary, or literary influences."[35] Yet it must also be emphasized that this is a *relative* trustworthiness, for "just because they serve the purpose of preaching, these stories could not be told in a neutral fashion; they must meet the requirements of the hearer, support and prove the message. Thus they were introduced with an underlying motive and intended for a definite purpose."[36]

The tales and legends are less historical than paradigms because of their very nature. Tales, however, are not all on the same level historically. They arose in three different ways: by extending paradigms, by introducing foreign motifs, and by borrowing foreign material; and the historical judgment upon a tale is related to its origin. A historical basis is to be presupposed when the tale developed from a paradigm. Only when a non-Christian story is the probable origin of a Christian tale is the historical reliability of the narrative really brought into question. Even legends must *not* be ruled out as possible vehicles of history, for legends too may contain some historical content.

In general, Dibelius is confident of the trustworthiness of the sayings. In various ways, he says, "we can see that Jesus'

[34]Martin Dibelius, *Jesus,* trans. Charles B. Hendrick and Fredrick C. Grant (Philadelphia: Westminster, 1949).
[35]Dibelius, *From Tradition to Gospel,* p. 61.
[36]*Ibid.,* p. 62.

sayings were handed down with great fidelity, thanks to the unencumbered memory of his unspoiled followers and to their reverence for their Master's word."[37] He suggests that "it is proper to speak of nongenuine sayings only where the later circumstances, conditions, or problems of the already existing Church are clearly presupposed."[38] The sayings having to do with Jesus' rank and fate, for example, must be evaluated carefully from the historical perspective for "the communities could not hand on presentiments of Jesus' rank, and hints of his fate, without giving expression to what they now knew, after the issue, about Jesus' rank and now, thanks to the Easter faith, understood about Jesus' fate."[39] Dibelius concludes that in general the sayings of Jesus may be relied upon as historical, yet he warns that the historian would do well to look at the tradition as a whole and not build too much upon an individual saying if it does not cohere with the rest of the tradition.

According to Dibelius, then, the narratives and sayings may be used with proper critical care in a study of Jesus. This he proceeds to do in his book as he discusses Jesus' particular historical and religious background, and examines the general features of the movement among the masses led by Jesus, a Galilean prophet and holy man. In the rest of the book Dibelius deals with Jesus' teaching concerning himself and his relationship to God; Jesus' basic principles for life in the kingdom; the forces which opposed Jesus and brought about his death; and the witness of the church to his resurrection. Dibelius's use of form criticism in a study of Jesus results in a rather full and confident presentation of the earthly Jesus.

Bultmann and the Life of Jesus

Bultmann's analysis of the Gospel tradition, along with his other theological and historical presuppositions, gives a particular slant to his views on reconstructing a history of the earthly Jesus. He is skeptical about the possibility of historical research into the life of Jesus and seriously doubts the legitimacy of such a study.

Bultmann's view of the nature of the *narrative* tradition

[37]Dibelius, *Jesus,* p. 25.
[38]*Ibid.,* p. 26.
[39]*Ibid.,* p. 28.

35

makes him skeptical of its historicity. Of course, he does not doubt that Jesus lived and did many of the *kinds of works* attributed to him in the tradition. But he is skeptical about the report of any specific activity being a historical report and is quite sure that the narrative material in the tradition cannot give us insight into the life and personality of Jesus. "I do indeed think that we can now know almost nothing concerning the life and personality of Jesus, since the early Christian sources show no interest in either, are moreover fragmentary and legendary; and other sources about Jesus do not exist."[40] Bultmann gives assurance that "the doubt as to whether Jesus really existed is unfounded and not worth refutation. No sane person can doubt that Jesus stands as founder behind the historical movement whose first distinct stage is represented by the oldest Palestinian community. But how far that community preserved an objectively true picture of him and his message is another question."[41]

Bultmann is not as skeptical of the sayings as he is of the narratives. "Little as we know of his life and personality, we know enough of his *message* to make for ourselves a consistent picture."[42] Yet the sayings in the tradition as well as the narratives go back to the Christian community which both passed on actual sayings of Jesus and placed its own teachings on the lips of Jesus. How is it possible to distinguish between the actual teachings of Jesus and those teachings which were put into his mouth by the church or modified by the church? The knowledge that the Synoptic Gospels were composed in Greek within the Hellenistic community, while Jesus and the oldest Christian group lived in Palestine and spoke Aramaic, helps in the process. "Everything in the synoptics which for reasons of language or content can have originated only in Hellenistic Christianity must be excluded as a source for the teaching of Jesus."[43] It cannot be supposed that all of the material thus retained goes back to Jesus, however, for there was an Aramaic-speaking Palestinian church after the time of Jesus. So, within the Palestinian material different layers must be dis-

[40]Rudolf Bultmann, *Jesus and the Word,* trans. Louise Pettibone Smith and Erminie Huntress Lantero (New York: Scribner's, 1958), p. 8.
[41]*Ibid.,* p. 13.
[42]*Ibid.,* p. 12.
[43]*Ibid.,* p. 13.

tinguished. Whatever materials show the specific interest or the church or reveal characteristics of later development must be rejected as secondary. An oldest layer is thus determined, although it can be determined with only relative exactness. Even this oldest layer *may* not go back to Jesus. "Naturally we have no absolute assurance that the exact words of this oldest layer were really spoken by Jesus. There is a possibility that the contents of this oldest layer are also the result of a complicated historical process which we can no longer trace."[44]

Bultmann's work on Jesus, therefore, is really a treatment of the message of Jesus, and "Jesus" here, according to Bultmann, actually refers to the complex of ideas in the oldest layer of the Synoptic tradition. Bultmann says, "By the tradition Jesus is named as bearer of the message; according to overwhelming probability he really was." But Bultmann suggests that "whoever prefers to put the name of 'Jesus' always in quotation marks and let it stand as an abbreviation for the historical phenomenon with which we are concerned, is free to do so."[45]

The comprehensive form critical studies of Dibelius and Bultmann and their application of form criticism to the life and teachings of the earthly Jesus continue to influence studies today. The discipline and its application to the life of Jesus have been modified by the work of scholars following Dibelius and Bultmann, however, and the following chapter will treat the scholarly evaluation and use of form criticism following the earliest work in the field.

[44]*Ibid.*
[45]*Ibid.*, p. 14.

III

Early Scholarly Evaluation
and Use of Form Criticism

New Testament scholars differed widely in their reaction to form criticism. Some scholars continued to emphasize source criticism, accepting Mark as history, and virtually ignored form criticism. Others defended the *basic* historicity of Mark and the other sources of the Synoptic Gospels but were increasingly affected by form criticism. Others accepted more completely the principles of form criticism, but those who accepted the principles differed in their application of the method.

CONTINUED USE OF SOURCE ANALYSIS ALONE

B. H. Streeter has been mentioned as the source critic who summed up the results of the scientific study of the Gospels to his day in a great book, *The Four Gospels: A Study of Origins.* Streeter first published his work in 1924 and took no account of the work of form criticism. The analysis of sources was his object, and he saw the analysis of sources as extremely important in several respects. It assists in the study of the authorship, date, and locality of origin of the Gospels. But more important, it also enables us to evaluate the Gospels as "historical authorities for the life of Christ."[1] Streeter feels that the range of sources (Mark, Q, M, and L) used by the Gospel writers very materially broadens the base for a historical study

[1]Streeter, *The Four Gospels: A Study of Origins,* p. 22.

of the life and teachings of Jesus and that the Gospels themselves must be seen as generally reliable historical documents because of the sources used by the Gospel writers.

The year before Streeter's book appeared, A. C. Headlam published a work, *The Life and Teachings of Jesus the Christ,*[2] which utilized the results of the analysis of the sources of the Gospels. Headlam sees himself as a defender of the "general credibility of the traditional account of the life and work of our Lord" against a school of critics which, while accepting Jesus as a real person and founder of Christianity, holds that "the greater part of the contents of the Gospel tells us not what He taught, but what the Christian Church which grew up after His death thought."[3]

Headlam had studied ancient history and was convinced that, if proper historical documents are used in accordance with the rules of historical method, then reasonably certain historical results may be obtained. His evaluation of the Gospels as authorities for the life and teachings of Jesus and his use of the sources illustrate the procedure which many were to follow. The historical value of Mark is derived from the fact that it was written by John Mark, the companion of both Paul and Peter, who had ample opportunity of acquiring knowledge of the life of Jesus. The source behind the sayings common to Matthew and Luke (Q) can be reconstructed with a fair degree of certainty, and it gives much information of the greatest importance. The historical accuracy of Luke and Matthew is not really subject to doubt according to Headlam. We know two of their sources, Mark and Q. We know that they were good sources, and that Luke and Matthew used them well. We may assume the same of other sources. Headlam concludes then that there are four independent sources, and that gradually, from all of the sources, the story of the life and teachings of Jesus can be constructed. Nothing should be ruled out on a priori grounds; nothing should be discarded to begin with. The various elements should be combined as the work is carried on.

[2]Arthur C. Headlam, *The Life and Teaching of Jesus the Christ* (2nd ed.; London: John Murray, 1927).
[3]*Ibid.,* p. ix.

CHALLENGES TO FORM CRITICISM

Although Streeter and Headlam wrote *after* the work of men like Wrede, Schweitzer, Schmidt, Dibelius, and Bultmann, they were still basing their work upon nineteenth century presuppositions. After the work of the earliest form critics, however, it could not simply be presupposed that Mark was essentially a historical presentation of Jesus of Nazareth which, when supplemented from the other sources, would represent a reliable history of the life and teachings of Jesus. Such a thing must be *proved*, and the basic postulates of the form critics must be disproved. It is not surprising, therefore, that scholars attempted to refute the postulates which would deny to them the use of the sources as authorities for reconstructing a life of the earthly Jesus.

In 1932 C. H. Dodd challenged the assumption of form criticism regarding "The Framework of the Gospel Narrative."[4] In particular, he dealt with the work of K. L. Schmidt. Dodd acknowledged that "Professor Schmidt seems to have made out his case that the main stuff of the Gospel is reducible to short narrative units, and that the framework is superimposed upon these units."[5] Dodd denied, however, that the order of the units is arbitrary and that the framework is only an artificial construction.

According to Dodd, three different types of materials are evidenced in Mark: independent units, larger complexes of materials, and an outline of the entire ministry of Jesus. Evidence of an outline of the entire ministry, of course, was the major interest of Dodd. Dodd put together some of the generalizing summaries which Schmidt saw used in Mark to link together the separate episodes (these include 1:14–15, 21–22, 39; 2:13; 3:7b–19; 4:33–34; 6:7, 12–13, 30) and found that the so-called generalizing summaries give a continuous outline narrative of the Galilean ministry. This is not accidental, nor is it the work of the Gospel writer himself, else the framework and the units used in the framework would fit better than they do. "Now if you have in hand a set of pictures, and desire to

[4] This is the title of an article by Dodd appearing in *Expository Times*, 43 (1932), 396–400. It was reprinted in *New Testament Studies* (New York: Scribner's, 1952), pp. 1–11.
[5] Dodd, *New Testament Studies*, p. 3.

frame them, you construct a frame to fit the pictures; but if you have in hand a set of pictures *and a frame,* not designed to fit one another, you must fit them as best you can, and the result may be something of a botch."[6] The "botch" seen in the Gospel of Mark is evidence that Mark had a traditional outline or frame with which he attempted to work. Dodd moved from the evidence in Mark itself to show that it is not intrinsically improbable that an outline of the ministry of Jesus in chronological order would be transmitted in the oral tradition. The primitive kerygma in Acts 10:37–41 and 13:23–31, for example, gives fragments of an outline of the life of Jesus.

Dodd suggested that Mark attempted to present all of his materials within the traditional outline but the outline was at the same time too meager and too broad. It was far too limited to provide a setting for all of the narratives, but it also referred to some phases of the ministry for which Mark had no detailed narratives. In addition, some of the materials at Mark's disposal were already partially grouped topically instead of chronologically. Dodd suggested that Mark solved this problem by a compromise between a chronological and topical order.

The conclusion Dodd drew is that "we need not be so scornful of the Marcan order as has recently become the fashion . . . there is good reason to believe that in broad lines the Marcan order does represent a genuine succession of events within which movement and development can be traced."[7] But it is clear that Dodd acknowledged a great measure of the presupposition of Schmidt and the form critics as far as the nature of the tradition is concerned. Even if it is acknowledged that Dodd proved his point (and this is not generally acknowledged), the Gospel of Mark cannot be used as history in the same way that it was before the advent of form criticism. Dodd himself admitted that "we shall not place in it [Mark] the implicit confidence it once enjoyed."[8]

T. W. Manson, a noted English New Testament scholar and teacher, whose career continued until his death in 1958, remained throughout his lifetime much more confident of the

[6]*Ibid.,* p. 9.
[7]*Ibid.,* p. 11.
[8]*Ibid.*

41

historicity of the Gospel tradition than did the form critics. Manson's first and most important work, *The Teaching of Jesus*,[9] is an admirable study of Jesus' teaching from the perspective of source analysis. It was first published in 1931 and it was written as if form criticism did not exist. In later lectures and essays Manson supported the critical presuppositions used in this work. He justified the use of the Gospels as "respectable historical material" and attacked the arguments of the form critics one by one.

Manson's reaction to the view that the framework of Mark was artificially constructed to contain the independent units of the tradition was simple: "The title of the Marcan framework to be regarded as respectable historical material is as good as that of any detailed story in the Gospel."[10] In light of Manson's general defense of the authenticity of the Marcan framework, it is important to note his grudging concession to the form critics. He admitted that "it is no longer possible to regard the Marcan framework, in all its details, as a rigid and unalterable scaffolding, into which everything must somehow be fitted. . . . Many concessions may have to be made to the disruptive criticism of Mark."[11]

Manson also disputed the idea that the church *created* the tradition in its present form to serve its needs. He scored the form critics for not seeing that early Christians could have preserved and selected stories of Jesus not merely to meet their needs but because of "plain admiration and love for their hero."[12]

Manson's overall judgment on form criticism is that the discipline should deal strictly with the *form* of the various units. "In fact if Form-criticism had stuck to its proper business, it would not have made any real stir. We should have taken it as we take the forms of Hebrew poetry or the forms of musical composition."[13] Manson's defense of the pre-form critical approach to the Synoptic Gospels was based on judg-

[9]T. W. Manson, *The Teaching of Jesus: Studies of its Form and Content* (2nd ed.; Cambridge: Cambridge University Press, 1935).
[10]T. W. Manson, *Studies in the Gospels and Epistles* (Philadelphia: Westminster, 1962), p. 6.
[11]*Ibid.*, p. 26.
[12]*Ibid.*, p. 6.
[13]*Ibid.*

ments which were at least as subjective as the presuppositions of the form critics. His arguments persuaded only those who needed no persuasion, and, indeed, Manson's grudging concessions seen here and there really serve to underline the need for a broad application of the method of form criticism to the Synoptic tradition.

More recently two Scandinavian scholars, Harald Riesenfeld and Birger Gerhardsson, have attempted to prove false the postulate upon which the discipline of form criticism most depends, that the formation of the material took place in the later Christian community. They attempt to demonstrate that Jesus delivered fixed material, both teachings and narratives, to his disciples to hand down to others.

Harald Riesenfeld stated the basic arguments in an address delivered at the opening session of the congress on "The Four Gospels in 1957" at Oxford.[14] He admits that form critics had made some permanent achievements in their research: they made a formal analysis of the individual units in the Gospel material. These units originally circulated in an oral form but were eventually written down, first in small groups of independent units and then in our Gospels. The elements of tradition were influenced by the life of the church which passed them on or gave them their final written form. But Riesenfeld holds that when form criticism went further and explained the *beginning* of the Gospel tradition by the activity of the early church it went astray. He asserts that the original source of the Gospel tradition was not preaching, catechetical instruction, or controversy, but that "the beginning of the Gospel tradition lies with Jesus himself."[15] Riesenfeld attempts to establish this by identifying the origin and transmission of the Christian tradition with the origin and transmission of Jewish tradition. In Jesus' day Jewish tradition was transmitted in accordance with firmly established laws. There was not a vague, uncontrolled diffusion of stories, tales, and anecdotes, but a rigorously controlled transmission of material from a master to a specially chosen student. The rabbi passed on a body of material fixed in content and form, and he watched

[14]Harald Riesenfeld, *The Gospel Tradition and its Beginnings: A Study in the Limits of "Formgeschichte"* (London: A. R. Mowbray, 1957).
[15]*Ibid.*, p. 23.

over the approved pupils to see that it was memorized well. "The ideal pupil was one who never lost one iota of the tradition."[16]

Riesenfeld relates the method of transmitting Jewish tradition to the Christian community by using Paul's writings to show that Paul was the bearer of a Gospel tradition, that Paul was carefully taught a Christian tradition. He suggests that the time spent by Paul in Jerusalem with Peter after the three years in Arabia was used in the examination of Paul. The chief concern of these weeks was the testing of Paul by Peter to see "whether he, Paul, during his term of preparation, had really made the tradition of the words and deeds of Jesus his own, in the form, that is, which these words and deeds had assumed by that date."[17]

This "holy tradition," according to Riesenfeld, was not used primarily in the missionary preaching or the community instruction, although the mission preaching pointed and led to it and the instruction presupposed it and related itself to it. The traditional material was used in the Christian assemblies, for it was conceived of as a New Torah (law) and it was used as the Torah was used in Judaism.

The tradition, the New Torah, comes from Jesus himself. The fact that the tradition about Jesus possessed a special character as Holy Word in the early church can be explained only by the fact that this tradition was derived from Jesus himself. Not only is this true of the teachings of Jesus, it is also true of the tradition of Jesus' deeds, for "there are indications . . . which lead to the conclusion that Jesus also spoke with his disciples about deeds and their significance."[18]

Some significant qualifications to his thesis are added by Riesenfeld. His claim, he says, is not that the Gospel tradition existed from the very first just as it is in the Synoptic tradition, or that it can be traced back to Jesus as it now stands. "It is self-evident that the moulding of the tradition—e.g. by the collecting and grouping of individual pericopes, through its transformations and also through its additions—came about gradually in the life of the primitive Church."[19]

[16]*Ibid.*, p. 18.
[17]*Ibid.*, p. 19.
[18]*Ibid.*, p. 26.
[19]*Ibid.*, p. 27.

A pupil of Riesenfeld, Birger Gerhardsson, in his book *Memory and Manuscript*, carried forward Riesenfeld's work by presenting in great detail the evidence from Judaism and early Christianity which supports their case.[20] The first half of the book is a helpful discussion of how both written and oral Torah was transmitted in Judaism. The second half of the book uses the writings of Paul, Luke, and the early church fathers to try to find evidence of a transmission of tradition in early Christianity similar to that in Judaism

The theory that Jesus taught his disciples in such a way as to ensure a mechanical transmission of the tradition ignores the probability that Jesus did not envision the interval between his death and parousia (second coming) that the later church envisioned. It also ignores the unquestioned influence of the resurrection faith upon the tradition, and the part played by Christian prophets in the transmission of the material. Moreover, it fails to explain sufficiently the variant reports of single sayings of Jesus which are contained in the Gospels. If Jesus made his disciples learn the sayings by heart, why the different forms? Even if the existence of a "Christian rabbinate" were established (and it is certainly not established by Riesenfeld and Gerhardsson), there is no guarantee that the entire Synoptic tradition in its present form goes back to the earthly Jesus. Form criticism is still a necessary method for studying the Synoptic tradition.

CAUTIOUS USE OF FORM CRITICISM

Cautious acceptance and use characterized the attitude and practice of most New Testament scholars regarding form criticism. This was true of American and particularly of English New Testament scholars. Burton Scott Easton was one of the earliest American scholars to have evaluated form criticism. In December, 1927, he gave a series of lectures at the General Theological Seminary, New York, in which he dealt with form criticism.[21]

Some of the units of the tradition, in the estimation of

[20]Birger Gerhardsson, *Memory and Manuscript: Oral Tradition and Written Tradition in Rabbinic Judaism and Early Christianity,* trans. Eric J. Sharpe (Lund: C. W. K. Gleerup, 1961).
[21]Burton Scott Easton, *The Gospel Before the Gospels* (New York: Scribner's, 1928).

Easton, may be classified as to form. The form known to Dibelius as paradigm and to Bultmann as apophthegm is an obvious form; the miracle story is also a "definite type of story with abundant parallels throughout the ancient world everywhere";[22] and the parable is a highly distinctive form of teaching. But attempts to classify other narrative and teaching material have not proved helpful, and form critics violate the "rule" when they classify in any way other than by form. "When Dibelius speaks of 'myths,' for instance, he violates this rule, for the myth has no set form of any kind. The name describes not the outward structure but the contents of a narrative."[23]

The value of discovering the form is not nearly so great in the estimation of Easton as it is in the estimation of Dibelius and Bultmann. The very form which a narrative takes, paradigm and tale, for example, is taken by Dibelius to indicate date and historical value. But Easton, while agreeing that there are different tendencies in the paradigms and tales, says, "Neither need be the outgrowth of the other, . . . why might not the preacher, the storyteller, and the teacher be one and the same person?"[24] Form criticism as a tool to establish the history of the tradition, therefore, has a very limited utility. "It can tell us that the manner of phrasing is conventional, and it can explain the conventions. It can tell us why a certain wording was used, why certain details were added or omitted. And it can tell us—within limits—something of the use to which the material was put. But the study of forms *as forms* cannot carry us further."[25] The discipline of form criticism "cannot give us even the relative ages of the special forms it identifies, and the absolute ages lie totally beyond its reach. Nor can it aid our historical estimate of the contents of any story."[26]

Although Easton denies that form criticism as such is historical criticism, he does not deny the validity of the historical criticism engaged in by the form critics. Indeed "form-criticism may prepare the way for historical criticism."[27] Easton

[22]*Ibid.*, p. 67.
[23]*Ibid.*, pp. 61–62.
[24]*Ibid.*, p. 80.
[25]*Ibid.*
[26]*Ibid.*, pp. 80–81.
[27]*Ibid.*, p. 81.

sets forth a method of determining whether the sayings attributed to Jesus in the Synoptic tradition were spoken by Jesus himself or originated in the early church. Beliefs certainly held by the early church are to be isolated. "Then, if we find these freely placed in his mouth by the Synoptists, we must agree that the tradition is largely of apostolic creation. If, on the other hand, we find that our witnesses are chary of seeking such authentication for their own beliefs, we are equally bound to conclude that the tradition was carefully guarded."[28] Easton concludes that "where beliefs of the Synoptic period can be distinguished with certainty from the teachings of Jesus, we find the former more scantily supported by sayings placed in his mouth,"[29] and that as far as the sayings are concerned "the primary historic value of the Synoptists is not for their own age but for the tradition of the teachings of Jesus."[30]

The *narratives* as well as sayings go back not to the early church but to the earthly Jesus, in the view of Easton. When it is remembered that discipleship in the movement initiated by Jesus had a personal emphasis, that the disciples were personal believers in Jesus, even "the so-called 'mythical' sections in the tradition cease to be a problem."[31] At the most the stories simply "heighten the impression that the Jesus of history actually produced."[32]

Vincent Taylor very cautiously evaluated form criticism as a legitimate tool in lectures given at the University of Leeds in 1932.[33] He does not see the discipline as a totally negative tool at all. In fact, he declared, "Form-Criticism seems to me to furnish constructive suggestions which in many ways confirm the historical trustworthiness of the Gospel tradition."[34]

It is obvious that Taylor has to modify the basic postulates and procedures of the earliest exponents of form criticism in

[28]*Ibid.*, p. 88.
[29]*Ibid.*, p. 109.
[30]*Ibid.*
[31]*Ibid.*, p. 162.
[32]*Ibid.*
[33]Vincent Taylor, *The Formation of the Gospel Tradition* (London: Macmillan, 1933; 2nd ed., 1935).
[34]*Ibid.*, p. vi. In the preface to the second edition Taylor says that form criticism does not weaken the judgment of F. C. Burkitt that Mark gives the chief outlines of Jesus' career and that it "embodies the private reminiscences of Peter, supplemented for the last week by the reminiscences of the young Mark himself." *Ibid.*, p. ix.

order to come to his conservative results. Although he is in basic agreement that the earliest tradition consisted of small isolated units, he finds evidence of longer connected blocks of material and affirms that Mark is no "formless collection," although "the outline is less complete than has been supposed" by earlier critics.[35] Taylor traces the historical materials in the Gospel back to eyewitnesses. The influence of eyewitnesses must be qualified; everything in Mark's Gospel does not go back to Peter's testimony. "But when all qualifications have been made, the presence of personal testimony is an element in the formative process which it is folly to ignore."[36] If the form critics who deny the influence of eyewitnesses are right, in the opinion of Taylor, "the disciples must have been translated to heaven immediately after the Resurrection."[37]

Taylor's view of the *origin* of the tradition differs from the view of Dibelius and Bultmann. The church did not *originate* the tradition although it did take the recollections of the words and deeds of Jesus and apply them to its needs. The practical needs of daily life, the necessity of understanding and explaining the faith, and the necessity of defending the faith "would kindle recollections and prompt the relating of His words and deeds in the first assemblies."[38] As the church did not originate the tradition, it did not greatly alter the tradition. At times an "ideal" element entered into the tradition, circumstances were misunderstood, and words of Jesus colored by ideas and beliefs of those passing along the tradition. But "what is this beyond that which we might reasonably expect? . . . A reconstruction which implies the untrustworthiness of the greater part of the tradition is wanting in probability and is not just to the Gospel records."[39]

Some "forms" in the tradition are found by Taylor, but he does not feel that all of the materials can be analyzed on the basis of forms. The paradigm or apophthegm is a form "in which oral tradition naturally clothes itself."[40] But Taylor is not satisfied with the names used by Dibelius and Bultmann.

[35]*Ibid.*, p. 41.
[36]*Ibid.*, p. 43.
[37]*Ibid.*, p. 41.
[38]*Ibid.*, p. 37.
[39]*Ibid.*, p. 38.
[40]*Ibid.*, p. 29.

"*Paradigmen* . . . is too general and is too exclusively associated with the theory that the stories were formed under the influence of preaching," and "*apophthegmata* is literary rather than popular and, by concentrating attention too much on the final word of Jesus, it almost invites a depreciatory attitude to the narrative element."[41] Taylor suggests the term "Pronouncement-Stories." This leaves the possibility of origin open and it emphasizes the main element, a pronouncement of Jesus on some aspect of life, belief, or conduct. Taylor also sees good reason to assume the existence of another popular narrative form, called "miracle stories" by Bultmann and "tales" by Dibelius. He chooses to use Bultmann's term "miracle stories."

The general expression "Stories about Jesus" is used by Taylor for the remaining narratives about Jesus, for the material has no definite structural form. Although there is no one narrative form for these stories about Jesus, the narratives do have some common characteristics. "In almost all cases Jesus stands in the centre and usually secondary characters are not named or described. Conversations take place between two persons, or between Jesus and a group; in a few stories only, like the Penitent Thief, are three speakers introduced."[42] Taylor suggests that these speeches show that practical aims rather than narrative interests were responsible for the formation of the stories. He also suggests that the formative process of the stories about Jesus is more one of shortening than one of embellishment. Since "this is exactly what ought to be the history of genuine historical tradition . . . the result . . . of a study of the formal aspect of the Stories about Jesus is to strengthen confidence in their historical value."[43]

Little justification is found for Bultmann's classification of the sayings of Jesus into proverbs, prophetic and apocalyptic sayings, laws and community regulations, "I sayings," and parables. "The terms do little more than describe stylistic features; they do not denote popular forms into which an individual or a community unconsciously throws sayings."[44] The parable, however, is a form which is important. Taylor sees parables as circulating orally, singularly or in pairs, and later

[41]*Ibid.*, p. 30.
[42]*Ibid.*, p. 166.
[43]*Ibid.*
[44]*Ibid.*, p. 31.

collected. Introductions were added by the evangelists and sayings of similar character added to the original parables. But Taylor is very critical of Bultmann's skepticism of the authenticity of the parables, and in general Taylor is more confident of the authenticity of the Synoptic sayings than Dibelius or Bultmann. He acknowledges that there was a creative power of the community and that the tradition has been influenced in its transmission. But "substantially the sayings tradition is historically trustworthy," and "the tradition of the words of Jesus is far better preserved than we have any right to expect, and with much greater accuracy than is to be found in the record of the words of any great teacher of the past."[45] "A limited tool" is Taylor's evaluation of form criticism. But he reminds us that a tool is something to be used, whatever its limitations may be.

Form criticism received a champion in England in R. H. Lightfoot at the University of Oxford. Although Lightfoot disclaims the title of "champion" of the claims of form criticism, in the Bampton Lectures of 1934 he introduced the insights of the form critics to his countrymen,[46] and in this series of lectures and later works he applied the method to the Gospel of Mark.

In a later work Lightfoot questioned whether form criticism "will help us to draw nearer to the central Figure of the gospels, in His historical manifestation."[47] This is true because the church preserved the tradition not primarily for historical interests but for religious interests. The most valuable aspect of form criticism, then, is the way it seeks to relate the individual stories to the life of the church which preserved them and used them to give its message to the world. "In this way the gospels can be to us . . . within limits which need to be carefully guarded, a mirror of the hopes and aspirations, the problems and the difficulties, of the early Church."[48]

The fact that the tradition had virtually no order and arrangement before being set down in the Gospels brought

---

[45]*Ibid.*, pp. 110, 113.
[46]Robert Henry Lightfoot, *History and Interpretation in the Gospels* (London: Hodder and Stoughton, 1935).
[47]Robert Henry Lightfoot, *The Gospel Message of St. Mark* (Oxford: Clarendon Press, 1950), p. 105.
[48]*Ibid.*, p. 102.

Lightfoot to ask what the writers sought to convey by their selection and arrangement of the material. This question placed more emphasis upon the personality and intention of the individual evangelists than had earlier form critics, and Lightfoot's interest in the total purpose of the evangelists led him to apply form criticism to the Gospels in a different way than the earlier scholars. The purpose of Mark, according to Lightfoot, is not simply or chiefly biographical; it is doctrinal. Although Mark deals with history and contains materials which are important in a study of the life of Jesus, his chief purpose is "to show the history in the light in which he himself sees it, and wishes his readers also to regard it . . . to interpret the history and to set forth . . . its meaning and significance."[49] Lightfoot became a pioneer in yet another method of Gospel study, redaction criticism.

THE STUDY OF PARABLES: A PRODUCTIVE USE OF FORM CRITICISM

The ultimate judgment on form criticism comes from its value for a study of the Synoptic tradition and the life of Jesus. The application of the method of form criticism to the parables by C. H. Dodd and Joachim Jeremias has proved particularly productive. These men combined form criticism with insights growing out of earlier work on the parables, especially the attempts to define carefully the exact nature of the parables of Jesus.

Before the modern critical period of biblical study, parables were interpreted as allegories; but Adolf Jülicher challenged this approach decisively in a work climaxing earlier critical labors and serving as a landmark for Dodd, Jeremias, and all later scholars.[50] Jülicher denied that the parables are allegories in any sense. The different people, events, and other items in the stories of Jesus do not refer to realities outside of the stories. The individual items are not symbols which demand interpretation. The stories are similitudes, comparisons drawn by Jesus from daily life to make his message plain and vivid. Jülicher also emphasized that a parable has *one* point of comparison, and his actual method tended to make the point of

[49]Lightfoot, *History and Interpretation in the Gospels*, p. 98.
[50]A. Jülicher, *Die Gleichnisreden Jesu* (2 vols.; Tübingen: J. C. B. Mohr, 1888, 1899).

each parable a general religious truth. Concerning the mean-ing of the parable of the talents, for example, Jülicher says, "We must vote for the broadest possible application, fidelity in all that God has entrusted to us."[51] The parable of the sower leads to the judgment that much labor may be lost and yet a good harvest may be reaped in any kind of religious work. The parable of the hidden treasure teaches that one should always sacrifice a lower good for a higher. The parable of the waiting servants teaches that one should be prepared for emer-gencies. The parable of the lamp and bushel teaches that eventually truth will out.[52]

C. H. Dodd accepts the conclusion of Jülicher that parables are not basically allegories; but he warns that too rigorous a distinction must not be made, for in a parable of any length "it is likely that details will be inserted which are suggested by their special appropriateness to the application intended, and if the application is correctly made by the hearer, he will then see a secondary significance in these details."[53] But the true parable is not strictly an allegory and any such details are strictly subordinate to the major emphasis of the story and do not destroy the unity of the story. Dodd acknowledges that "Jülicher and his followers, then, have done great service in teaching us how to take the first step towards the understand-ing of the parables. It is to accept the story as a piece of real life, and form our judgment upon it."[54]

Dodd does not follow the view of Jülicher, however, that the meaning of a parable is a broad, religious generalization. The parables must bear upon the *actual* situation in which Jesus taught and the applications, therefore, must be related to the *particular* settings in which the stories were delivered. The interpreter must discover the setting of a parable and the *specific* application which would suggest itself to a person who was in that particular situation. Dodd, therefore, tries to estab-lish "the general orientation of the teachings of Jesus" so that we might have the context in which the parables are to be placed. The kingdom of God is established by Dodd as the

[51]Quoted in C. H. Dodd, *The Parables of the Kingdom* (rev. ed.; New York: Scribner's 1961), p. 12.
[52]*Ibid.*, pp. 12–13.
[53]*Ibid.*, p. 9.
[54]*Ibid.*, p. 12.

general theme of Jesus' message and therefore as the logical general context for the parables. A glance at the parables themselves supports this conclusion. Many parables are introduced with a formula which mentions the kindom of God, and others which do not use the formula are definitely related to the kingdom. Jesus' understanding of the kingdom, then, is shown by Dodd to be essential to the study of the parables. This understanding of the kingdom may be gained through explicit and unambiguous teachings and then applied to the parables. Dodd concludes from this study that

> ... in the earliest tradition Jesus was understood to have proclaimed that the Kingdom of God, the hope of many generations, had at last come. It is not merely imminent; it is here. . . . The sayings which declare the Kingdom of God to have come are explicit and unequivocal. They are moreover the most characteristic and distinctive of the Gospel sayings on the subject. They have no parallel in Jewish teaching or prayers of the period. If therefore we are seeking the *differentia* of the teaching of Jesus upon the Kingdom of God, it is here that it must be found.[55]

The individual parables must be interpreted within the context of Jesus' proclamation of the *presence* of the kingdom, and the specific teaching of each parable must be related to Jesus' distinctive view of the kingdom. Some help may be given by the framework within which a parable was passed down and within which it is contained in the Gospels, but it may well be that the present application of the parable is not original and gives us no help. In some cases "we may have confidence that the application of the parable came down with the parable itself in the earliest tradition," but "on the other hand there are grounds for suspecting that in many cases the application was not a part of the earlier tradition, but was supplied by the evangelist, or by his immediate authority."[56]

We may ascertain which parables have been passed down with their original applications in the light of the relationship of the application to the actual situation in Jesus' day. The parable of the children in the market place (Matt. 11:16–19 and parallel passage, Luke 7:31–35), for example, has an application relating the parable to the frivolous attitude of the

[55]*Ibid.*, pp. 33–34.
[56]*Ibid.*, p. 16.

Jews to Jesus and to John. "There is no good reason for doubting this application. If in the ministry of Jesus the Kingdom of God comes, as in the ministry of John its coming had been heralded, then our attention is drawn to the egregious folly of such childish behaviour in the presence of the supreme crisis of history."[57]

Illustrative of parables which have been reapplied is a series of parables of crisis (the faithful and unfaithful servants, Matt. 24:45-51 and parallel passage, Luke 12:42-46; the waiting servants, Mark 13:33-37 and parallel passage, Luke 12:35-38; the thief at night, Matt. 24:43-44 and parallel passage, Luke 12:39-40; and the ten virgins, Matt. 25:1-12). In their present context in the Gospels they refer to the second advent of Christ and are used as exhortations to be prepared for that crisis. Dodd feels that here definitely are parables which have been reapplied by the church because the church's situation, not Jesus' situation, is presupposed by the parables. The early church saw itself as living in the interval between two crises, the incarnation and the second advent; but the sayings of Jesus were uttered in a different context, in the context of a brief period of intense crisis—the crisis of the coming of God's kingdom. The church reapplied the parables with both homiletical and eschatological motives: it gave "a general and permanent application to sayings originally directed toward an immediate and particular situation" and gave to sayings "which were originally associated with the historical crisis of the past, an application to the expected crisis of the future."[58]

In the case of the parables which have been reapplied, such as the parables of crisis, we must carefully scrutinize the parable itself, and attempt to relate it to the complex of ideas in the minds of Jesus and his hearers and to Jesus' interpretation of his own ministry which is reconstructed by his explicit and unambiguous sayings in the tradition. When the parables of crisis are freed from their artificial context and interpreted in light of Jesus' mission and message, it will be seen that they were originally intended to enforce Jesus' appeal to men "to recognize that the Kingdom of God was present in all its momentous consequences, and that by their conduct in the presence of this tremendous crisis they would judge themselves as

[57]*Ibid.*, p. 88.
[58]*Ibid.*, p. 105.

faithful or unfaithful, wise or foolish."[59] However, when the crisis had passed, "they were adapted by the Church to enforce its appeal to men to prepare for the second and final world-crisis which it believed to be approaching."[60]

Joachim Jeremias also applies form critical principles to the parables in a productive way. He feels that with the parables one "may be confident that he stands upon a particularly firm historical foundation. The parables are a fragment of the original rock of tradition."[61] Jeremias, writing twelve years after Dodd's work on the parables, acknowledged his debt "for stimulus and instruction to C. H. Dodd's fundamentally important book."[62] Although he does feel that the one-sided nature of Dodd's conception of the kingdom—the emphasis on the kingdom as present (realized eschatology)—resulted in an unwarranted contraction of the eschatology in Jesus' teachings and colored Dodd's interpretation of the parables, Jeremias is confident that Dodd's approach will result in "nothing less than a return . . . to the very words of Jesus himself."[63]

The major contribution of Jeremias is to carry out Dodd's methodology in a detailed and comprehensive way, to "dot the i's and stroke the t's of Dodd's exposition."[64] In doing this Jeremias finds definite principles of transformation of the parables by the church which must be counteracted before a return to Jesus is possible. When the laws of transformation are applied to the parables and the influence of the primitive church counteracted, "the total impression of the parables has been immensely simplified. . . . Many parables express one and the same idea by means of varying symbols." The different elements in the parables which conveyed different messages when the parables were read allegorically are seen to be secondary. "As a result, a few simple essential ideas stand out with increasing importance. It becomes clear that Jesus was never tired of expressing the central ideas of his message in constantly changing images."[65]

[59]*Ibid.*, pp. 138–39.
[60]*Ibid.*
[61]Joachim Jeremias, *The Parables of Jesus*, trans. S. H. Hooke (rev. ed. tr. of 6th German ed.; New York: Scribner's, 1963), p. 11.
[62]*Ibid.*, p. 9.
[63]*Ibid.*
[64]A. M. Hunter, *Interpreting the Parables* (London: SCM, 1960), p. 39.
[65]Jeremias, *The Parables of Jesus*, p. 115.

Thus, as we have seen in this chapter, the world of New Testament scholars came slowly and cautiously to an acceptance of the basic presuppositions of the form critics and the necessity and validity of a study of the Synoptic tradition in its preliterary period by form criticism. Students of Bultmann, of course, maintained his skeptical view of the authenticity of the tradition and his skeptical methodology in studying the tradition. The skepticism of Bultmann caused American and especially English scholars to be wary of the discipline which was associated almost exclusively with the name of Bultmann, and the limitations of form criticism as such were stressed by these men. Yet, form criticism proved to be a useful tool, particularly in the study of the parables by such non-Bultmannians as C. H. Dodd and Joachim Jeremias. Moreover, the antagonism between the Bultmann school and those who disagreed with Bultmann's negation of the life of the earthly Jesus was altered radically after the middle of the twentieth century. The following chapter shows developments in form criticism among the "post-Bultmannians" which have affected every student of the Gospels and of the life of Jesus.

IV

Form Criticism and the
Current Quest for the
Historical Jesus

During the nineteenth century, scholars used the results of Gospel research to attempt a reconstruction of the life
of Jesus. The possibility of such a work was presupposed; only
the correct procedure needed to be found and followed. From
the beginning of the twentieth century, however, two basically
different approaches are discernible. One group of scholars
represented by C. H. Dodd, T. W. Manson, and Vincent Taylor, continued the original quest. They rejected the possibility
of a complete "biography," but they did feel that a "life" of
Jesus with a broad chronology was possible. Another group,
influenced more strongly by the form critics in general and by
Rudolf Bultmann in particular, gave up the quest completely.
Bultmann had concluded that a quest of the historical Jesus as
carried out in the nineteenth century was *impossible* because
of the nature of the sources. But just as important in bringing
scholars to give up the quest was Bultmann's judgment that
such a quest was unnecessary and indeed *illegitimate* since the
object of Christian faith is not the historical Jesus. Interest in
the historical Jesus was taken by Bultmann to be an illegitimate
clinging to this-worldly props for faith, a desire for an objec-
tive verification of faith. The real Christ event, however, is the
church's proclamation. We cannot and must not use the "proclamation" as a "source" to reconstruct the "historic Jesus" with
his "messianic consciousness," his "inwardness," or his "heroic
character." This is the "Christ according to the flesh" who belongs to the past. "It is not the historic Christ who is the Lord,

57

but Jesus Christ as he is encountered in the proclamation."[1] There was, therefore, a lack of interest in the history of Jesus on the part of Bultmann; and the scholars following Bultmann rejected the quest of the historical Jesus in even a modified way.

THEOLOGICAL AND HISTORICAL DEVELOPMENTS INFLUENCING THE CURRENT QUEST

Today there continues to be an interest in the historical Jesus among non-Bultmannian scholars, though their research has been modified by the results of critical scholarship, including form criticism. What is surprising, however, is that a "new quest" of the historical Jesus has developed among the disciples of Bultmann. If a date can be given for the beginning of this new quest it is October 20, 1953, when Ernst Käsemann gave a lecture on "The Problem of the Historical Jesus"[2] at a reunion of students of Bultmann. Käsemann acknowledged that the Gospels were not written to give mere historical information about Jesus. The New Testament presents Jesus as the Lord of the believing community, "*not* as he was in himself, *not* as an isolated individual."[3] Käsemann even questions whether the formula "the historical Jesus" is appropriate or legitimate, because "it is almost bound to awaken and nourish the illusion of a possible and satisfying reproduction of his 'life story.'"[4]

The fact that the New Testament is not concerned merely with Jesus as an isolated individual but as Lord of the community, however, does not permit the question about the Jesus of history to be ignored. Primitive Christianity itself was not minded to "allow myth to take the place of history nor a heavenly being to take the place of the Man of Nazareth. . . . Primitive Christianity is obviously of the opinion that the earthly Jesus cannot be understood otherwise than from the far side

---

[1]Bultmann expressed this opinion in an essay on "The Significance of the Historical Jesus for the Theology of Paul" in 1929, reprinted in *Glauben und Verstehen,* 1 (2nd ed.; 1954), 208. Quoted from Stephen Neill, *The Interpretation of the New Testament* 1861–1961 (New York: Oxford, 1964), p. 271.
[2]In English translation in Ernst Käsemann, *Essays on New Testament Themes,* trans. W. J. Montague (London: SCM, 1964), pp. 15–47.
[3]*Ibid.,* p. 23.
[4]*Ibid.*

of Easter, that is, in his majesty as Lord of the community and that, conversely, the event of Easter cannot be adequately comprehended if it is looked at apart from the earthly Jesus."[5] Likewise, the fact that the materials of the tradition do not give enough information to weave "the fabric of a history in which cause and effect could be determined in detail"[6] should not lead to a complete lack of interest in the earthly Jesus. Ignoring the earthly Jesus indicates a failure to take seriously the primitive Christian concern with the identity between the exalted and humiliated Lord and overlooks the fact that "there are still pieces of the Synoptic tradition which the historian has to acknowledge as authentic if he wishes to remain an historian at all."[7] The concern of Käsemann in his address was "to show that, out of the obscurity of the life story of Jesus, certain characteristic traits in his preaching stand out in relatively sharp relief, and that primitive Christianity united its own message with these."[8]

The theological *necessity* of a new quest, then, grows out of the proclamation of the church itself. The Gospel is not just the story of the earthly Jesus, but it is not just the proclamation of a mythological—preexistent and exalted—Lord.

James M. Robinson says, "It is this concern of the *kerygma* [proclamation] for the historicity of Jesus which necessitates a new quest. For how can the indispensable historicity of Jesus be affirmed, while at the same time maintaining the irrelevance of what a historical encounter with him would mean, once this has become a real possibility due to the rise of modern historiography?"[9] A position maintaining the irrelevancy of the results of the quest "cannot fail to lead to the conclusion that the Jesus of the *kerygma* could equally well be only a myth, for one has in fact declared the meaning of his historical person irrelevant."[10]

Other students of Bultmann followed the lead of Käsemann. Ernst Fuchs concentrated upon Jesus' message as evidenced in

[5]*Ibid.*, p. 25.
[6]*Ibid.*, p. 45.
[7]*Ibid.*, p. 46.
[8]*Ibid.*
[9]James M. Robinson, *A New Quest of the Historical Jesus* (London: SCM, 1959), p. 88. (Hereafter cited as *A New Quest.*)
[10]*Ibid.*

his action. Jesus' conduct as a whole gives evidence of who he is. His conduct and teaching imply an understanding of his relation to God. This implicit understanding becomes explicit in the kerygma of the church.[11] Gerhard Ebeling asked, "Who shall forbid us to ask the question concerning the historic Jesus? This defeatism has no justification . . . either as regards the state of the actual historical sources available to us or in relation to the possibility of historical understanding in general."[12] Günther Bornkamm pressed the question, "How could faith of all things be content with mere tradition, even though it be that contained in the Gospels? It must break through it and seek behind it to see the thing itself. . . . It cannot be seriously maintained that the Gospels and their tradition do not allow enquiry after the historical Jesus. Not only do they allow, they demand this effort."[13] The new quest has met with a favorable response not only among the students of Bultmann but also among a variety of scholars in different countries with different theological and critical presuppositions.

Rudolf Bultmann responded to the new questers in a paper read before the Heidelberg Academy of Sciences on July 25, 1959.[14] He declared that he had not denied the continuity between Jesus and the kerygma. The continuity is between the historical Jesus and the primitive proclamation, not between the historical Jesus and the Christ. "The Christ of the kerygma is not a historical figure which could enjoy continuity with the historical Jesus. The kerygma which proclaims him is a historical phenomenon, however. Therefore it is only the continuity between the kerygma and the historical Jesus which is involved."[15] The kerygma presupposes the historical Jesus; without the historical Jesus there would be no kerygma. But, Bultmann said, the kerygma only presupposes the fact that

[11]Ernst Fuchs, *Studies of the Historical Jesus*, trans. Andrew Scobie (London: SCM, 1964), pp. 11–31.
[12]*Zeitschrift für Theologie und Kirche* (1959), Additional number, p. 20. Quoted in Neill, *The Interpretation of the New Testament*.
[13]Günther Bornkamm, *Jesus of Nazareth*, trans. Irene and Fraser McLuskey with James M. Robinson (London: Hodder and Stoughton, 1960), pp. 9, 22.
[14]Rudolf Bultmann, "The Primitive Christian Kerygma and the Historical Jesus," *The Historical Jesus and the Kerygmatic Christ*, ed. and trans. Carl E. Braaten and Roy A. Harrisville (New York: Abingdon, 1964), pp. 15–42.
[15]*Ibid.*, p. 18.

Jesus was, and it is not interested in the content and character of Jesus' history. The use of historical research to legitimize the kerygma is a denial of the nature of the kerygma.

Bultmann's refusal to let the Christ of the kerygma be colored by the concrete picture of the earthly Jesus is supported by a statement in his address in 1959:

It is often said, most of the time in criticism, that according to my interpretation of the kerygma Jesus has risen in the kerygma. I accept this proposition. It is entirely correct, assuming that it is properly understood. It presupposes that the kerygma itself is an eschatological event, and it expresses the fact that Jesus is really present in the kerygma, that it is *his* word which involves the hearer in the kerygma. If that is the case, then all speculation concerning the modes of being of the risen Jesus, all the narratives of the empty tomb and all the Easter legends, whatever elements of historical fact they may contain, and as true as they may be in their symbolic form, are of no consequence. To believe in the Christ present in the kerygma is the meaning of the Easter faith.[16]

Bultmann's disinclination to enter into the new quest has not halted the project. However, the reservations expressed by Bultmann have influenced the work of other scholars. A careful distinction is made between the various kinds of information in the New Testament, and care is taken in describing the exact significance of the historical knowledge of Jesus. James M. Robinson, for example, had declared that "modern historiography mediates an existential encounter with Jesus, an encounter also mediated by the *kerygma*."[17] Although the historical Jesus does not prove that the kerygma is true, Robinson said, the historical Jesus does confront us with "action and a self which, like the exorcisms, may be understood either as God's Spirit (Mark 3.29; Matt. 12.28), or Beelzebub (Mark 3.22), or insanity (Mark 3.21). The historical Jesus confronts us with existential decision, just as the *kerygma* does."[18] After Bultmann's 1959 statement, however, Robinson reformulated his position and dropped much of the emphasis on an encounter with the historical Jesus through modern historiography. Christians are to proclaim not the historical Jesus but the kerygma, but it is also important to implement the claim

[16]*Ibid.,* p. 42.
[17]Robinson, *A New Quest,* p. 90.
[18]*Ibid.,* p. 77.

of the kerygma to be proclaiming a risen Lord who is identi-
fied with the earthly Jesus by participating in the present critical historical study of Jesus. According to Robinson's later
formulation, the historical study of Jesus is not of the basic
task of preaching but in our situation it is necessary for the
well-being and improvement of preaching.[19]

Norman Perrin, a scholar who comes to the quest as a
student of T. W. Manson and Joachim Jeremias, finds it helpful, following Bultmann, to distinguish between three different kinds of knowledge: historical knowledge, historic knowl-
edge, and faith-knowledge. Historical knowledge is the objec-
tive factual knowledge concerning the earthly Jesus. " 'Historical knowledge' of Jesus of Nazareth might be held to include
the fact that he accepted his death as the necessary consequence of his proclamation of the Kingdom, and of his 'table-
fellowship of the Kingdom' with 'tax collectors and sinners',
and that he went to the cross with a sure confidence that it
would ultimately serve, and not hinder, the purpose of God."
This kind of knowledge is not unique to Jesus. It is similar to
the knowledge that "Socrates accepted his death as a necessary consequence of his own innermost convictions, and drank
the hemlock with a serenity arising out of the courage of those
convictions."[20]

Historic knowledge is historical knowledge which becomes
significant to us in our present situation. The historical knowledge of how Jesus accepted the cross can become historic
knowledge if it assumes a direct significance for the present
time. Again, historic knowledge is not unique to Jesus. The
historical knowledge of Socrates' acceptance of the hemlock
may become historic knowledge.

Faith-knowledge is "knowledge of Jesus of Nazareth which
is significant only in the context of specifically Christian faith,
i.e. knowledge of him of a kind dependent upon the acknowl-
edgement of him as Lord and Christ."[21] Faith-knowledge
moves beyond historic knowledge because special worth is attributed to the person concerned and knowledge of that per-

[19]James M. Robinson, "The Recent Debate on the New Quest," *Journal
of Bible and Religion*, 30 (1962), 207.
[20]Norman Perrin, *Rediscovering the Teaching of Jesus* (New York:
Harper and Row, 1967), p. 236.
[21]*Ibid.*, p. 234.

son assumes more than historic significance. For the Christian, it is possible to say, "Christ died for my sins in accordance with the scriptures," but this is not the result of historical research—it depends upon recognition of Jesus as the Christ, as the one who bestows well-being (or salvation) on one.

The historical knowledge which we can gain from the Gospels cannot mediate an existential encounter with Jesus, but it is significant to faith. "In a tradition which 'believes in Jesus', historical knowledge can be a source for the necessary content of faith . . . without thereby becoming the main source of that content."[22] The main source, of course, is the proclamation of the church, "a proclamation arising out of a Christian experience of the risen Lord."[23] Knowledge of the historical Jesus can also "act negatively as a check on false or inappropriate faith-images, or aspects of a faith-image."[24] Because the claim of the Christian church is that the risen Lord is none other than the earthly Jesus, "we may and we must use such historical knowledge of Jesus as we possess to test the validity of the claim of any given form of the Church's proclamation to be *Christian* proclamation."[25] Perrin also declares that historical knowledge of the teaching of Jesus is relevant for modern Christians. If a modern believer responding to the proclamation of the church stands in a relation to God parallel to the ancient disciple who responded to the proclamation of the earthly Jesus, then the teaching of Jesus to the disciple is also applicable to the modern believer. Of course, the practical problems remain of crossing the barrier of two thousand years and a quite different world view. But Jesus' teachings are important for Christian faith and life.

PRESUPPOSITIONS AND
METHOD OF CONTEMPORARY SCHOLARS

The scholars who are engaged in the current quest agree by and large upon a set of presuppositions and a method which makes a study of the earthly Jesus possible. The work of the source critics is accepted: Mark was the earliest Gospel and was used by Matthew and Luke along with another source

[22]*Ibid.*, p. 244.
[23]*Ibid.*
[24]*Ibid.*, p. 246.
[25]*Ibid.*, pp. 247–48.

(Q) which is basically a sayings source earlier than Mark. Matthew and Luke each also had a unique source or sources. But the material now written in the Gospels existed earlier in an oral form in independent units (except for the passion narrative), and the overall framework in which the units now exist is a creation of the Gospel writers. The oral tradition passed through or was created by the church as it developed from an Aramaic-speaking Palestinian community.

The presuppositions of modern scholars, then, demand that the independent unit be the beginning point of study. Source criticism must first be applied to the unit of tradition. When a unit occurs in all three Synoptic Gospels, Mark is to be taken as the earliest written form of that unit, and attention may be limited to Mark's version of the tradition. When a unit of the tradition occurs in Q, the unit may be carried back even further. But it is necessary to reconstruct the original Q form from the later forms in Matthew and Luke. At times the Matthean form of the Q unit is more original and at times the Lukan form is more original. The tendencies of the two Gospel writers must be considered as the more original form of Q is determined. It is incorrect, however, to assume that a unit in Mark and/or Q is necessarily more primitive than a unit in the material unique to Matthew or to Luke since all of the material passed successively through Palestinian and Hellenistic stages. Source criticism, then, may assist in determining the earliest written form of a unit. Source criticism may also assist in a limited way in verifying the historicity of tradition. Since the sources may be regarded as relatively independent, when the content of a unit is repeated in two or more sources, the possible authenticity of the tradition may be regarded as being increased.

Once the unit has been studied from the perspective of the written sources, form criticism in its strictest sense is applied to the unit of tradition. The history of the tradition must be traced to determine the earliest form of the unit. Sayings of Jesus, for example, passed successively through the Palestinian church, the Jewish Hellenistic church, and into the Gentile Hellenistic church. Additions and modifications of the later church must be seen and deleted. The tendencies in the transmission of the material must be discounted. The method of Dibelius and Bultmann as modified by later studies is the method used at this point. The principles of the transformation of the parables by the church outlined in detail by Jeremias are helpful in a study of the tradition. The test of multiple attestation found helpful in a study of the sources helps here also, for when a teaching or purportedly historical fact occurs in more than one form the possible authenticity of that teaching or fact is increased. If, for example, a piece of factual information occurs in a paradigm, parable, and isolated saying, it may be assumed that the fact was not created for the forms but existed before the forms were created.

What next? It cannot be assumed that the earliest form of the unit of tradition which has been studied with the methods of source and form criticism is authentic. The unit may go back to Jesus, but it may come from the church which transmitted the tradition. How may we distinguish between authentic and inauthentic material?

Joachim Jeremias, who never completely gave up the earlier quest of the historical Jesus, has joined with the scholars who are engaged in the current quest and gives suggestions which may help distinguish between authentic and inauthentic material. He warns that the current quest is different from the quest of the nineteenth century. "Our aims have become more modest, because the mistakes of the 'classical' quest of the historical Jesus serve as warnings to us not to want to know more than we can know; that is already a point of inestimable worth."[26] Jeremias stresses two tests to distinguish between authentic and inauthentic material. If a saying attributed to Jesus has Aramaic traits it may be considered authentic; if a saying reflects the Palestinian world it may be considered authentic. Of course, the sayings of Jesus himself would have been spoken in Aramaic and would reflect Palestinian conditions, but so would sayings of the Palestinian church after Jesus. Jeremias himself admits, "It must of course be remembered that the earliest Christian community spoke Aramaic too; so not every Aramaism is evidence of authenticity. At any rate, however, we are drawing nearer to Jesus himself when we succeed in rediscovering the pre-Hellenistic form of the

[26]Joachim Jeremias, *The Problem of the Historical Jesus,* trans. Norman Perrin (Philadelphia: Fortress, 1964), p. 15.

tradition."[27] Jeremias's linguistic and environmental criteria must be applied along with other tests, but applied in conjunction with these other criteria they prove to be very valuable in rediscovering the historical Jesus.

Rudolf Bultmann, in his treatment of the parables, gave criteria which enable us to judge that a saying is authentic. "We can only count on possessing a genuine similitude of Jesus where, on the one hand, expression is given to the contrast between Jewish morality and piety and the distinctive eschatological temper which characterized the preaching of Jesus; and where on the other hand we find no specifically Christian features."[28] This may be stated positively in a form which is found useful by all students of the earthly Jesus: we may be sure that sayings attributed to Jesus are authentic when they differ from contemporary Judaism or from the proclamation of the church. This criterion of dissimilarity or distinctiveness is, of course, a criterion which leads to minimal rather than to maximal results. Jesus could have used much from the Old Testament and the Judaism of his day, and much of the teaching useful to the early church could well have come from Jesus himself. But students of the new quest judge that it is safer to follow the skeptical methodology than to accept everything that is in doubt. Reginal Fuller says that "on some points Jesus *could* have agreed with the post-Easter church" and that "Jesus might also have quoted or used with approval Rabbinic teaching." Yet, this skeptical method provides a safer course than a principle of accepting whatever tradition may be doubtful. "It may result in a reduction of the available historical data, but at least it should be reliable enough as far as it goes; and actually it turns out that it does go far enough for our purposes."[29]

Another criterion, a criterion of consistency or coherence, was suggested by C. E. Carlston to compensate for the negative aspect of the criterion of dissimilarity or distinctiveness.[30] Bultmann's criterion of distinctiveness helps with the tradition

[27]*Ibid.*, pp. 17–18.
[28]Bultmann, *History of the Synoptic Tradition*, p. 205.
[29]Reginald H. Fuller, *The New Testament in Current Study* (New York: Scribner's, 1962), p. 33.
[30]Charles Edwin Carlston, "A *Positive* Criterion of Authenticity?" *Biblical Research*, 7 (1962), 33–44.

comparable with the teachings of contemporary Judaism **and** the early church; but what of the material which cannot **be** so tested? Carlston suggests that material which cannot **be** tested by the criterion of distinctiveness be judged as authentic if it "will fit reasonably well into the eschatologically based demand for repentance that was characteristic of Jesus' message, and . . . will reflect or fit into the conditions (social, political, ecclesiastical, linguistic, etc.) prevailing during the earthly ministry of Jesus, rather than (or, in some cases, as well as) conditions which obtained in the post-resurrection church."[31] This criterion can be applied only *after* the central message of Jesus has been established by other criteria. The criterion may be stated thus: Material may be accepted as authentic if it is consistent with the material established as authentic by the test of distinctiveness.

EXAMPLES OF THE APPLICATION OF FORM CRITICISM

A number of critical works on the life and teaching of Jesus have been produced by scholars using some form of the procedure outlined above. The scope and method of modern form criticism will be illustrated through some of these works. An early new quest treatment of Jesus was given by Günther Bornkamm.[32] It is instructive to compare Bornkamm's work with Bultmann's *Jesus and the Word* which appeared thirty years earlier. Bultmann confined his presentation to Jesus' "word" and even here he confessed that "Jesus" means the message of the oldest layer of the Synoptic tradition which may not be the message of the earthly Jesus—although Bultmann believed that it was. Bornkamm acknowledges that it is impossible to attempt critically a detailed description of the course of Jesus' life biographically and psychologically. But he declares that in the tradition "the person and work of Jesus, in their unmistakable uniqueness and distinctiveness, are shown forth with an originality which again and again far exceeds and disarms even all believing understandings and interpretations. Understood in this way, the primitive tradition of Jesus is brim full of history."[33] Hence Bornkamm, after a discussion

[31]*Ibid.*, p. 34.
[32]Bornkamm, *Jesus of Nazareth.*
[33]*Ibid.*, p. 26.

of the relationship between faith and history in the Gospels and the cultural and religious environment of Jesus, offers a chapter in which he tries "to compile the main historically indisputable traits, and to present the rough outlines of Jesus' person and history."[34]

Although "the childhood and adolescence of Jesus are obscure for us from the historical point of view," we may assert that "the home of Jesus is the semi-pagan, despised Galilee. His native town is Nazareth. His family certainly belonged to the Jewish part of the population which, since the times of the Maccabees had reattached themselves to the temple cult in Jerusalem and the legal practices of Judaism." He was the son of Joseph the carpenter. Mary was his mother and we know the names of his brothers. Jesus' mother tongue was the Aramaic of Galilee, and the scene of his ministry was small towns like Bethsaida, Chorazin, and Capernaum.[35]

Jesus' baptism by John is "one of the most certainly verified occurrences of his life." We cannot say how long Jesus' ministry lasted, but "we learn a great deal about his preaching, the conflict with his opponents, his healing and the additional help he granted the suffering, and the powerful influence which went forth from him. The people flock to him. Disciples follow him, but his enemies also arise and increase." The tradition allows us to see that "the last decisive turning point in his life is the resolution to go to Jerusalem with his disciples in order to confront the people there with his message in face of the coming kingdom of God. At the end of this road is his death on the cross." Bornkamm declares that "these meagre, indisputable facts comprise a very great deal. There is little enough in this enumeration, and yet it contains most important information about the life story of Jesus and its stages."[36]

Reginald H. Fuller subjected the miracles of Jesus to a form critical study in his work *Interpreting the Miracles*.[37]

---

[34]*Ibid.*, p. 53.
[35]*Ibid.*, pp. 53–54.
[36]*Ibid.*, pp. 54–55. In addition to the one chapter consisting of a personality sketch of Jesus, Bornkamm devotes one chapter each to a discussion of Jesus' disciples and Jesus' journey to Jerusalem resulting in suffering and death. The remainder of the book is given to the teaching of Jesus.
[37]Reginal H. Fuller, *Interpreting the Miracles* (Philadelphia: Westminster, 1963).

After discussing the biblical concept of miracle as sign of "the intervening action of God" rather than "something that happens contrary to nature," Fuller asks, "Did Jesus do miracles?" The rabbinic *Tractate Sanhedrin* affirms that Jesus was charged with practicing sorcery, and "supports the claim that Jesus performed exorcisms."[38] An analysis of the sources also confirms the picture of Jesus as a miracle worker, for with the exception of the special Matthean material, all of the sources contain references to Jesus' healings.

The most valuable evidence for Jesus' healings, however, is the reference to exorcism and healing in Jesus' own words. "If these sayings are authentic, they contain pretty nearly first-hand evidence that Jesus did perform miracles."[39] Form criticism is therefore applied by Fuller to the sayings of Jesus. The Beelzebub saying is the best attested:

But if it is by the Spirit (Luke: finger) of God that I cast out demons, then the kingdom of God has come upon you (Matt. 12:28 and parallel passage, Luke 11:20).

This saying occurs in Q and is supported indirectly by Mark 3:22. Fuller applies the criteria of authenticity discussed earlier to the saying and finds that "it does not reflect the faith of the church, for it makes no explicit assertion that Jesus is Messiah. Moreover, it speaks of the Reign of God as already in some sense breaking in. So it is completely different from anything one would expect from Judaism, where the Kingdom of God was a purely future expectation." The saying, therefore, cannot have been attributed to Jesus by the church. "We may safely assume that it is a genuine saying of Jesus himself."[40]

Concerning Jesus' answer to John in Q:

The blind receive their sight and the lame walk, lepers are cleansed and the deaf hear, and the dead are raised up, and the poor have good news preached to them. And blessed is he who takes no offense at me (Matt. 11:5–6; Luke 7:22–23),

Fuller says that it is different from anything in contemporary Judaism and does not contain the explicit Christology of the

[38] *Ibid.*, p. 23.
[39] *Ibid.*, p. 25.
[40] *Ibid.*, p. 27.

early church, "so there is no reason why this too should not be an authentic saying of Jesus."[41]

The saying of the blessedness of the disciples (reconstructed from Luke 10:23–24 and Matthew 13:16–17),

Blessed are the eyes which see what you see,
 And the ears which hear what you hear;
For I tell you
 that many prophets and kings desired to see
  what you see,
 and did not see it;
 and to hear what you hear,
 and did not hear it,

has the "same strong consciousness of fulfilment which is lacking in Judaism and characteristic of Jesus, and the same absence of the explicit Christology of the post-resurrection church. The saying, therefore, satisfies the form-critics' criteria of authenticity."[42] Attention is also called by Fuller to the poetic structure of the saying characteristic of Aramaic verse. Luke 13:32 (L) ("Go and tell that fox, 'Behold, I cast out demons and perform cures today and tomorrow . . .'") also is a saying which is generally regarded as authentic. Fuller's conclusion is that "the evidence in favor of the general tradition of Jesus' exorcisms is little short of overwhelming."[43]

The actual narratives of Jesus' healings (both the miracles in the pronouncement stories and miracle stories proper) are approached from a form critical perspective by Fuller. He concludes that the narratives of Jesus' miracles came mainly from the Palestinian churches and are "ideal scenes." But he questions the idea that these ideal scenes are created out of nothing. "Is it not more likely that the early Christians drew upon their store of *generalized memory* about Jesus?"[44]—particularly since these stories originated in the Palestinian community. The possibility is not even ruled out that occasionally a story preserves the memory of an actual incident. In particular are mentioned Simon's mother-in-law (Mark 1:39–41), the paralytic (Mark 2:1–12), the Syrophoenician woman (Mark 7:24–30), blind Bartimaeus (Mark 10:46–53), and the

[41] *Ibid.*, p. 28.
[42] *Ibid.*
[43] *Ibid.*, p. 29.
[44] *Ibid.*, p. 32.

centurion of Capernaum (Matt. 8:5–13). Fuller sums it up by saying that the tradition that Jesus did perform exorcisms and healings (which may also have been exorcisms originally) is very strong, "but we can never be certain of the authenticity of any actual miracle story in the gospels. While a few of them may rest upon specific memory, most of them have probably been shaped out of generalized memories."[45]

The presupposition and methods of the current quest are also used by Fuller in *The Foundations of New Testament Christology*, a book concerned partly with "what can be known of the words and works of Jesus, and with what these words and works disclose about his own self-understanding."[46] The Synoptic tradition is full of "christologically impregnated material" which must be studied to determine Jesus' self-understanding. The bulk of the material consists of narration, however (the infancy narratives, the baptism, the miracle stories, the temptation, Peter's confession at Caesarea Philippi, the transfiguration, the passion narrative, the resurrection stories), and this fact makes our task of recovering the history of the earthly Jesus somewhat easier, for "on any view, these stories took shape after the resurrection." They reflect not Jesus' self-understanding but the christological beliefs of the post-resurrection church, hence, "it is not historical skepticism, but sound critical method to assign these stories in their present shape (whatever factual basis they may have) to the theology of the community."[47]

A small body of christological material in the Synoptic sayings of Jesus is left from which to discover Jesus' self-understanding. Fuller concentrates first on the more characteristic parts of Jesus' teaching to probe the self-understanding which that teaching implies. Jesus' proclamation of the kingdom, an event that is already happening precisely and concretely in his own work and words, implies a Christology. Jesus' call to decision, exorcisms and healings, ethical teaching, understanding of God, teaching about God's providential care, and understanding of his death (seen in Luke 13:32 and Mark 14:25, which pass the tests of authenticity), all imply a Christology.

[45]*Ibid.*, p. 39.
[46]Reginald H. Fuller, *The Foundations of New Testament Christology* (New York: Scribner's, 1965), p. 16.
[47]*Ibid.*, pp. 102–103.

The proclamation, teaching, and deeds of Jesus may *imply* a Christology but they are not directly christological. However, there are some sayings of Jesus in which a direct Christology is asserted. Fuller's treatment of some important sayings will illustrate his method of determining their authenticity.

"Messiah" (Greek: Christ) is an important term used by the church in interpreting the meaning of Jesus. In Jesus' day there were political and military messianic ideas in vogue among the Jews, and it is frequently asserted that Jesus divested the term "Messiah" of its Jewish associations, "spiritualized" it, and used it of himself. Fuller examines the Synoptic material to see if Jesus understood himself to be and taught that he was Messiah. The Q material has no sayings of Jesus with the "Christ" as a self-designation. Mark 9:41 is the only such passage in Mark: "For truly, I say to you, whoever gives you a cup of water to drink because you bear the name of Christ, will by no means lose his reward." But this verse is obviously secondary, dependent upon a saying which does not mention "Christ," such as Matthew 10:42: "And whoever gives to one of these little ones even a cup of cold water because he is a disciple, truly, I say to you, he shall not lose his reward." So Jesus did not explicitly claim to be Messiah, but there is one important passage in which the title "Christ" is given to Jesus by others and his reaction recorded. Can this passage, Mark 8:27–33, be used to support Jesus' acceptance of the title of Messiah?

[27]And Jesus went on with his disciples, to the villages of Caesarea Philippi; and on the way he asked his disciples, "Who do men say that I am?" [28]And they told him, "John the Baptist; and others say, Elijah; and others one of the prophets." [29]And he asked them, "But who do you say that I am?" Peter answered him, "You are the Christ." [30]And he charged them to tell no one about him.

[31]And he began to teach them that the Son of man must suffer many things, and be rejected by the elders and the chief priests and the scribes, and be killed, and after three days rise again. [32]And he said this plainly. And Peter took him, and began to rebuke him. [33]But turning and seeing his disciples, he rebuked Peter, and said, "Get behind me, Satan! For you are not on the side of God, but of men."

This passage has several elements in it: (1) Peter's confession, (2) a command to silence, (3) a prediction of the passion,

(4) a rebuke of Jesus by Peter and a rebuke of Peter by Jesus. Fuller shows that the command to silence is a typical Marcan theme, and it must be eliminated as an addition by Mark in keeping with the theme of the "Messianic Secret." The passion prediction in verse 31 must be credited to the church, and it cannot be taken as belonging originally to the passage. Verse 32 is to be credited to Mark, not to Jesus, for it forms a link between the passion prediction and the rebuke of Peter by Jesus. This leaves a pronouncement story consisting of three parts: the question of Jesus as to who they say he is; the answer of Peter, "You are the Christ"; and the pronouncement by Jesus, "Get behind me, Satan! For you are not on the side of God, but of men." Hence, Jesus rejects messiahship as "a merely human and even diabolical temptation."[48]

Fuller sees Jesus as conceiving of his ministry in terms of eschatological prophecy, so it is instructive to see how Fuller treats the material in the Synoptic Gospels which show Jesus as a prophet. Fuller establishes that some of Jesus' contemporaries regarded him as a prophet, even as a specific prophet *redivivus* (reborn). The report that Jesus was John the Baptist or Elijah *redivivus* occurs in Mark 6:14–15 and 8:28. Since there is no evidence that the church ever interpreted Jesus as John the Baptist *redivivus* or even as Elijah *redivivus*, "it would seem then that on traditio-historical grounds, Mark 6:14 and 8:28 should be taken as genuine historical reminiscence."[49] It has also been established that there were prophetic characteristics in the style and content of Jesus' ministry. Furthermore, sayings of Jesus in Mark 6:4 and Luke 13:13 compare the fate of Jesus with that of a prophet, and they clearly indicate that "he understood his role in prophetic terms in so far as it involved rejection and martyrdom."[50]

The heart of the question "Did Jesus understand himself as a prophet?" is arrived at in a collection of sayings in the Q material.

29"Woe to you, scribes and Pharisees, hypocrites! for you build the tombs of the prophets and adorn the monuments of the righteous, 30saying, 'If we had lived in the days of our fathers, we would not

[48]*Ibid.*, p. 109.
[49]*Ibid.*, p. 127.
[50]*Ibid.*

73

have taken part with them in shedding the blood of the prophets.'
[31]Thus you witness against yourselves, that you are sons of those
who murdered the prophets. [32]Fill up, then, the measure of your
fathers. [33]You serpents, you brood of vipers, how are you to escape
being sentenced to hell? [34]Therefore I send you prophets and wise
men and scribes, some of whom you will kill and crucify, and some
you will scourge in your synagogues and persecute from town to
town, [35]that upon you may come all the righteous blood shed on
earth, from the blood of innocent Abel to the blood of Zechariah
the son of Barachiah, whom you murdered between the sanctuary
and the altar. [36]Truly, I say to you, all this will come upon this
generation.
[37]"O Jerusalem, Jerusalem, killing the prophets and stoning those
who are sent to you! How often would I have gathered your children together as a hen gathers her brood under her wings, and you
would not! [38]Behold, your house is forsaken and desolate. [39]For I
tell you, you will not see me again, until you say, 'Blessed is he
who comes in the name of the Lord'" (Matt. 23:29–39).

In this collection of sayings Jesus ranges his own mission in
the prophetic succession. But are these sayings authentic? Do
they reflect Jesus' conviction concerning himself or the church's
conviction about Jesus? The church did interpret Jesus as the
Mosaic servant-prophet, and the alleged sayings of Jesus using
this category must be eliminated as church constructions. But
the sayings in Matthew 23 present Jesus as a prophet in more
general, non-Mosaic terms. "This material should not, therefore, be eliminated with the other titles as formations of the
post-Easter community."[51] These sayings, therefore, give us
important insight into Jesus' concept of himself. "The finality
of the judgments pronounced over Israel at the end of each of
these sayings (vv. 31, 36 and 38) indicates that Jesus thought
of his mission not only as belonging to the same class as that
of the OT prophets, but as representing the final prophetic
mission to Israel, and of his own rejection (and possible martyrdom) as the culmination of Israel's rejection of the word
of Yahweh."[52] These sayings show us that "Jesus thought of his
own mission not simply as one in the prophetic series, but as
the final mission, bringing God's last offer of salvation and
judgment."[53]

[51]Ibid., p. 126.
[52]Ibid., p. 129.
[53]Ibid.

Norman Perrin has studied the Synoptic tradition from the viewpoint of form criticism, and his book, simply entitled *Rediscovering the Teaching of Jesus*,[54] is a full-scale study of the teaching of Jesus. In some respects the work of Perrin is a continuation of the work of Jeremias (Perrin's teacher), for Perrin takes the kingdom of God as the central aspect of the teaching of Jesus and the parable as the major vehicle for the teaching. He places the parables in the context of Jesus' proclamation of the kingdom in first century Palestine and discovers the various aspects of the kingdom with which Jesus was concerned. But Perrin supplements the parables with numerous isolated sayings and similes of Jesus which serve to broaden the base for an understanding of Jesus' teaching and to sharpen the interpretation of specific teachings of Jesus. Perrin's treatment of several isolated sayings will illustrate his method.

Perrin studies Luke 11:20 and parallel passage, Matthew 12:28, to see what help it might give in understanding Jesus' teaching on the kingdom (cf. Fuller's view of this verse, above, page 69). He looks first at the larger setting and finds it to be at least as old as Q since both Matthew and Luke use the saying and setting, although in different ways. Is "finger" or "spirit" original? Since "spirit" is a favorite Lukan word it is difficult to conceive of him changing it to "finger," hence 'finger" must have been original.

Is the entire complex of sayings in Matthew 12:25–30 (Luke 11:17–23) original or have individual sayings been collected? Verses 27 and 28 may be omitted from the section and it reads much more smoothly and makes perfect sense. So the original tradition must have been Matthew 12:25, 26, 29, and 30, to which verses 27 and 28 were later added. Do verses 27 and 28 belong together originally? It seems inconceivable that they originally stood together since the connection of the two verses makes the work of the Jewish exorcists as much a manifestation of the kingdom as Jesus' exorcisms. Hence, Perrin arrives at an isolated saying existing originally in much the same form as it is in Luke 11:20: "But if it is by the finger of God that I cast out demons, then the kingdom of God has come upon you."

[54]Norman Perrin, *Rediscovering the Teaching of Jesus* (New York: Harper, 1967).

Did Jesus say it or is it a creation of the church? **Perrin** claims, with Bultmann, that the saying "is full of that feeling of eschatological power which must have characterized the activity of Jesus."[55] It cannot be attributed to contemporary Judaism or to the church, for the use of "kingdom of God" in reference to the eschatological activity of God and the use of the verb "to come" in connection with this are not characteristic of Judaism or of the early church. "Further, the relating of the presence of the Kingdom to the present experience of a man is an emphasis unparalleled in Judaism."[56] The conclusion then is that "Luke 11.20 represents a saying attributed to Jesus in the tradition, the authenticity of which may be regarded as established beyond reasonable doubt."[57]

This saying is very helpful in understanding Jesus' teaching on the kingdom, for "the claim of the saying is that certain events in the ministry of Jesus are nothing less than *an experience* of the Kingdom of God." The saying shows also that "the experience of the individual, rather than that of the people as a whole, has become the focal point of the eschatological activity of God. . . . This concentration upon the individual and his experience is a striking feature of the teaching of Jesus, historically considered, and full justice must be done to it in any interpretation of that teaching."[58]

Matthew 11:12 (and parallel passage, Luke 16:16) is an important saying:

Matthew 11:12	Luke 16:16
From the days of John the Baptist until now the kingdom of heaven has suffered violence, and men of violence take it by force.	The law and the prophets were until John; since then the good news of the kingdom of God is preached, and every one enters it violently.

This is a Q saying. Is the Matthean or Lukan form more original? The Lukan form gives evidence of being edited drastically by Luke: "The idea of one epoch ending with John and the phrase 'to preach the good news of the Kingdom of God' are both Lukan, and the 'everyone enters it violently' smooths out

[55]*Ibid.*, p. 64.
[56]*Ibid.*
[57]*Ibid.*, p. 65.
[58]*Ibid.*, p. 67.

the linguistic and theological problems of the Matthean say-ing."[59] Hence, the Matthean form is to be preferred as more original.

The saying reflects an estimate of John the Baptist, and the saying's authenticity can be judged by comparing it with the history of the tradition of John the Baptist in the church. The history of John the Baptist tradition in the church is the his-tory of a continuous *playing down* of the Baptist, and since the saying in Matthew 11:12 reflects a *high estimate* of John the Baptist, it is to be attributed not to the church but to Jesus. A high estimate of the Baptist and a dependence of Jesus upon the Baptist "are inconceivable as products of a Christian community concerned to exalt its Lord and engaged in rivalry with a Baptist sect."[60]

The saying, then, is an authentic saying of Jesus which "looks back upon the Baptist as one whose ministry marks the 'shift of the aeons'" and envisions "an aeon of conflict, of victory and defeat, of achievement and disappointment, of success and failure."[61] The saying may have been originally inspired by the fate of the Baptist and to this extent the present editorial setting may be correct. The saying confirms "that the time of God's activity as king is now, and that the form of this activ-ity can be envisaged in terms of conflict. But it also adds a strange, new note: the conflict can issue in defeat as well as victory. The outcome of the battle may be sure, but the casu-alties are going to be real, not sham."[62]

Scholars remain convinced that a full scale biography of Jesus cannot be written; but they are not generally skeptical today about the possibility of a historical study of the earthly Jesus. Although scholars are more confident of rediscovering the original teachings of Jesus, they have also used form criti-cism for recovering historical events in Jesus' life. Reginald H. Fuller, for example, has given a rather full outline of the au-thentic Jesus tradition in which he traces major events in the life of Jesus from the baptism to the burial, gives a detailed outline of the message of Jesus (his teaching on the kingdom,

[59]*Ibid.*, p. 75.
[60]*Ibid.*
[61]*Ibid.*, pp. 76–77.
[62]*Ibid.*, p. 77.

demand for radical obedience, and teaching about God), speci-
fies activities of Jesus, and even lists authentic teachings of
Jesus regarding his fate.[63] Fuller's outline of authentic narrative material shows the positive results achieved by the use of
form criticism in a study of events in the life of the earthly
Jesus.

Form criticism as carried out by scholars today is proving
to be a profitable and positive tool for a study of the Synoptic tradition and the life of Jesus. Its negative and skeptical
characteristics continue to be important because of the nature
of the tradition, but form criticism has succeeded in helping
us to determine a great many authentic elements in the Gospel tradition of the life and teachings of Jesus.

[63]Reginald H. Fuller, *A Critical Introduction to the New Testament*
(London: Duckworth, 1966), pp. 99–102.

Glossary

CHRISTOLOGY—A theological interpretation of the person and work of Christ.

DOGMA—A teaching or body of teachings concerning religion formally and authoritatively proclaimed by a church.

ESCHATOLOGY—A teaching concerning last things, the end of the world. *Apocalyptic* eschatology views the end as brought about by God's intervention, whereby he destroys the ruling powers of evil and restores the righteous to life in his kingdom.

EXISTENTIAL—Concerned with an individual as radically free and responsible. *See* Existentialism.

EXISTENTIALISM—A philosophy centered upon the analysis of the existence of individual human beings, stressing the freedom and responsibility of the individual, the uniqueness of an ethical or religious situation, and the subjective experience of an individual in that situation.

JEWISH CHRISTIAN—Relating to the primitive Christianity of the Jews. In the earliest period of the Christian movement, Jewish followers of Jesus Christ did not cease being Jews, but interpreted Jesus in light of their Jewish heritage.

KERYGMA—The apostolic preaching concerning Jesus Christ.

MESSIAH, *or* CHRIST—The Hebrew term "messiah" means "anointed one" and refers to the expected king and deliverer of the Jews. "Christ" is a translation into Greek of the Hebrew term "messiah."

SYNOPTIC GOSPELS—The first three Gospels of the New Testament, so called because they take a common view of the events in the life of the earthly Jesus.

TRADITION—The process of handing down information, beliefs, and customs from one generation to another *and* the information, beliefs, and customs thus handed down.

Annotated Bibliography

THE ORIGINS OF FORM CRITICISM

REIMARUS, HERMANN SAMUEL. *Von dem Zwecke Jesu und seiner Jünger: Noch ein Fragment des Wolfenbüttelschen Ungenannten.* Edited by GOTTHOLD EPHRAIM LESSING. Brunswick: G. E. Lessing, 1778. This was the largest and most important of the seven "fragments" of Reimarus published by Lessing anonymously in a journal. The second half of the book was published in English as *Fragments from Reimarus, Consisting of Brief Critical Remarks on the Object of Jesus and his Disciples as seen in the New Testament.* Edited by CHARLES VOYSEY. London: Williams and Norgate, 1879. Reprinted, Lexington, Kentucky: American Theological Library Association, 1962.

STRAUSS, DAVID FRIEDRICH. *Das Leben Jesu, kritisch bearbeitet.* 2 vols. Tübingen: C. F. Osiander, 1835, 1836. English translation of fourth edition (1840) by GEORGE ELIOT, *The Life of Jesus Critically Examined.* 3 vols. London: Chapman Brothers, 1846. Strauss shows that, generally speaking, John is out of the question as a source for historical understanding of Jesus.

BAUR, FERDINAND CHRISTIAN. *Kritische Untersuchungen über die kanonischen Evangelien.* Tübingen: L. F. Fues, 1847. Baur confirms the conclusion of Strauss that John possesses no historically valuable tradition about Jesus, but he stresses that John was not intended to be a historical account.

LACHMANN, KARL. "De Ordine narrationum in evangeliis synopticis," *Theologische Studien und Kritiken,* 8(1835), 570 ff. Lachmann concludes that, since Matthew and Luke agree with each other in order only when they have the same order as Mark, Mark reproduced the tradition closest to the original.

WEISSE, CHRISTIAN HERMANN. *Die evangelische Geschichte kritisch und philosophisch bearbeitet.* 2 vols. Leipzig: Breitkopf und Härtel, 1838. Weisse points out that Mark represents a document which was the common source for the narrative material of Matthew and Luke and theorizes that Matthew and Luke combined with this source another common source of sayings of Jesus.

WREDE, WILLIAM. *Das Messiasgeheimnis in den Evangelien. Zugleich ein Beitrag zum Verständnis des Markusevangeliums.* Göttingen: Vandenhoeck und Ruprecht, 1901. Second edition (unrevised), 1913. Third edition (unrevised), 1963. Wrede attempts to demonstrate that Mark was shaped by the dogmatic theory of the Messianic Secret, that the historical and dogmatic elements are combined in Mark by the claim that Jesus concealed the fact of his Messiahship.

SCHWEITZER, ALBERT. *Das Messianitäts-und Leidensgeheimnis. Eine Skizze des Lebens Jesu.* Tübingen und Leipzig: 1901. English translation by WALTER LOWRIE, *The Mystery of the Kingdom of God: The Secret of Jesus' Messiahship and Passion.* New York: Dodd, Mead, and Co., 1914.

———. *Von Reimarus zu Wrede.* Tübingen: Mohr, 1906. English translation by W. MONTGOMERY, *The Quest of the Historical Jesus.* London: A. and C. Black, 1910; paperback ed., New York: Macmillan, 1961. A record of the attempts from 1778 to 1901 to write a life of Jesus, demonstrating that scholars failed to reach the historical Jesus because they read their own ideals into the sources. Schweitzer emphasizes particularly that liberal scholars missed the eschatological and that Jesus was an apocalyptic fanatic who, disappointed in his expectation of God's intervention, attempted to force the eschaton by his own sufferings.

WEISS, JOHANNES. *Das älteste Evangelium.* Göttingen: Vandenhoeck und Ruprecht, 1903. Weiss treats Marcan sources and, although referring to the "Apostolic" source, anticipates the work of the form critics in that he sees the influence of the church on the development of the units of tradition.

WELLHAUSEN, JULIUS. *Das Evangelium Marci.* Berlin: G. Reimer, 1903.

———. *Das Evangelium Matthaei.* Berlin: G. Reimer, 1904.

———. *Das Evangelium Lucae.* Berlin: G. Reimer, 1904.

———. *Einleitung in die drei ersten Evangelien.* Berlin: G. Reimer, 1905. In these works on the Synoptic Gospels Wellhausen attaches great importance to the activity of the church in the formation of the primitive tradition and anticipates some of the work of the form critics.

GUNKEL, HERMANN. *Genesis.* Göttingen: Vandenhoeck und Ruprecht, 1901; seventh edition (a reprint of the third ed. of 1910), 1966. The introduction to Genesis was translated by W. H. CARRUTH and published as *The Legends of Genesis: The Biblical Saga and History.* New York: Schocken, 1964. Gunkel applies form criticism to the units of Genesis and provides a critical procedure for a study of the units of the Synoptic Gospels.

SCHMIDT, KARL LUDWIG. *Der Rahmen der Geschichte Jesu. Literarkritische Untersuchungen zur ältesten Jesusüberlieferung.* Berlin: Trowitzsch und Sohn, 1919. This book gave the final blow to faith in the Marcan framework. Schmidt isolated individual units from the framework and prepared the way for other scholars to classify and study the individual units and to study the contribution of the editor or author of the Gospel.

DIBELIUS, MARTIN. *Die Formgeschichte des Evangeliums.* Tübingen: J. C. B. Mohr, 1919. English translation of second German edition (1933) by BERTRAM LEE WOOLF, *From Tradition to Gospel.* New York: Charles Scribner's Sons, 1934. The third German edition (1959) contains an essay by G. Iber on form criticism since Dibelius. Dibelius applies Gunkel's principles to a study of the narrative material of the Synoptic tradition. In retrospect he is seen as a conservative form critic.

———. *Jesus.* Berlin: W. de Gruyter, 1939. English translation, *Jesus.* Translated by CHARLES B. HENDRICK and FREDERICK C. GRANT. Philadelphia: Westminster Press, 1949. An application of Dibelius' form critical method to a study of the life and teachings of Jesus.

BULTMANN, RUDOLF. *Die Geschichte der synoptischen Tradition.* Göttingen: Vandenhoeck und Ruprecht, 1921. Second (enlarged) edition, 1931. Third edition (reproduction of second edition with supplementary notes), 1958. English translation of third edition by JOHN MARSH, *History of the Synoptic Tradition.* New York: Harper and Row, 1963. This was the first study of the entire Synoptic tradition from the perspective of form criticism. Bultmann attempts to write the history of the tradition and to show the forces at work on the tradition as it was formed and transmitted. This book is basic to modern day form criticism.

———. *Die Erforschung der synoptischen Tradition.* Giessen: Töpelmann, 1925. English translation by FREDERICK C. GRANT, "The Study of the Synoptic Gospels," *Form Criticism: Two Essays on New Testament Research.* Edited by FREDRICK C. GRANT. New York: Willett, Clark and Co., 1934. This is a popular exposition of the method elaborated much more fully in the *History of the Synoptic Tradition.*

————. *Jesus*. Berlin: Deutsche Bibliothek, 1926. English translation by LOUISE PETTIBONE SMITH and ERMINIE HUNTRESS LANTERO, *Jesus and the Word*. New York: Charles Scribner's Sons, 1934; available in paperback, "Scribner Library," 1958. A treatment of the message of Jesus based on Bultmann's understanding of the history of the Synoptic tradition.

STREETER, BURNETT HILLMAN. *The Four Gospels: A Study of Origins*. London: Macmillan, 1924. Revised edition, 1930. A comprehensive summary of the results of the study of the Gospels to his day. His original contribution is the "four document" theory of Gospel origins.

EARLY SCHOLARLY EVALUATION AND USE OF FORM CRITICISM

FASCHER, ERIC. *Die formgeschichtliche Method*. Giessen: Töpelmann, 1924. A history and evaluation of form criticism as it had developed to 1924. Fascher stresses the limitations of form criticism and declares that form criticism itself does not establish the authenticity or lack of authenticity of units of the tradition.

EASTON, BURTON SCOTT. *The Gospel Before the Gospels*. New York: Charles Scribner's Sons, 1928. A cautious American introduction to form criticism. Like Fascher, he stresses the limitations of form criticism as a historical tool.

MANSON, T. W. *The Teaching of Jesus: Studies of its Form and Content*. Cambridge: Cambridge University Press, 1931. The study of Jesus' teachings based on the view that the earliest written sources are basically historical.

————. *Studies in the Gospels and Epistles*. Edited by MATTHEW BLACK. Philadelphia: Westminster Press, 1962. A collection of lectures of Manson given between 1939 and 1953. In these lectures Manson affirms his belief in the historicity of the Gospels.

DODD, C. H. "The Framework of the Gospel Narrative," *Expository Times*, 43 (1932), 396–400. Reprinted in *New Testament Studies*. New York: Charles Scribner's Sons, 1952. Dodd attempts to show that the arrangement of the units in Mark is based at least in part upon a traditional framework of the history of Jesus.

TAYLOR, VINCENT. *The Formation of the Gospel Tradition*. London: Macmillan, 1933. Second edition, 1935. A cautious introduction to form criticism which acknowledges its usefulness as a limited tool.

LIGHTFOOT, ROBERT HENRY. *History and Interpretation in the Gospels*. London: Hodder and Stoughton, 1935.

————. *Locality and Doctrine in the Gospels.* London: Hodder and Stoughton, 1938.

————. *The Gospel Message of St. Mark.* Oxford: Clarendon Press, 1950. In these works Lightfoot both introduces form criticism to the English-speaking academic world and begins to use the discipline to discover the theological message of the Gospel writers. This aspect of the discipline of form criticism has become known as "redaction criticism."

RIESENFELD, HARALD. *The Gospel Tradition and its Beginnings: A Study in the Limits of "Formgeschichte."* London: A. R. Mowbray and Co., 1957. Riesenfeld attempts to show that the Gospel tradition was derived from Jesus himself and that the tradition was passed down carefully as was the rabbinic tradition.

GERHARDSSON, BIRGER. *Memory and Manuscript: Oral Tradition and Written Transmission in Rabbinic Judaism and Early Christianity.* Translated by ERIC J. SHARPE. Lund: C. W. K. Gleerup, 1961. An attempt to support the thesis of Riesenfeld by a careful study of the transmission of the tradition in Judaism and of Christian sources which tell of the delivery of the Gospel tradition.

DODD, C. H. *The Parables of the Kingdom.* London: Nisbet, 1935. Revised edition, 1961. Dodd applies form criticism to the parables and achieves results which remain decisive for a study of the parables and teachings of Jesus. He establishes that the context in which the parables must be interpreted is the eschatological preaching of Jesus. The one-sided understanding of Jesus' eschatology as "realized eschatology" is a limitation of the work.

JEREMIAS, JOACHIM. *Die Gleichnisse Jesu.* Zurich: Zwingli Verlag, 1947. English translation of third German edition (1954) by S. H. HOOKE, *The Parables of Jesus.* New York: Charles Scribner's Sons, 1954. English translation of sixth German edition, 1963. A revised version abbreviated for the non-scholar published as *Rediscovering the Parables.* New York: Charles Scribner's Sons, 1966. An epoch-making application of Dodd's method to the Synoptic parables. The work of Jeremias gave great impetus to current research into the teaching of Jesus.

FORM CRITICISM AND THE CURRENT QUEST FOR THE HISTORICAL JESUS

KÄSEMANN, ERNST. "Das Problem des historischen Jesus," *Zeitschrift für Theologie und Kirche*, 51 (1954), 125–53. Translated into English by W. J. MONTAGUE as "The Problem of the Historical Jesus," *Essays on New Testament Themes.*

London: SCM Press, 1964, pp. 15–47. This essay began the renewed discussion of the question of the historical Jesus.

BORNKAMM, GÜNTHER. *Jesus von Nazareth*. Stuttgart: Kohlhammer, 1956. Translated into English from the third German edition (1959) by IRENE and FRASER MCLUSKEY with JAMES M. ROBINSON as *Jesus of Nazareth*. New York: Harper and Row, 1960. An early product of the post-Bultmannian movement. Bronkamm treats the *life* and teachings of Jesus for the general public.

FUCHS, ERNST. "Die Frage nach dem historischen Jesus," *Zeitschrift für Theologie und Kirche*, 53 (1956), 210–29. Translated into English by ANDREW SCOBIE as "The Quest of the Historical Jesus," *Studies of the Historical Jesus*. London: SCM Press, 1964, pp. 11–31. Fuchs emphasizes the relation between the historical Jesus and the preaching of the church from a post-Bultmannian perspective.

CONZELMANN, HANS. "Jesus Christus," *Religion in Geschichte und Gegenwart*. Tübingen: J. C. B. Mohr, 1959, III, 619–53. Conzelmann reviews the current situation in the life of Jesus research.

————. "Zur Methode der Leben-Jesu-Forschung," *Zeitschrift für Theologie und Kirche*, 56 (1959), 2–13. Translated into English by CARL E. BRAATEN and ROY A. HARRISVILLE as "The Method of the Life of Jesus Research," *The Historical Jesus and the Kerygmatic Christ: Essays on the New Quest of the Historical Jesus*. New York: Abingdon Press, 1964, pp. 54–68. Conzelmann treats the situation in the life of Jesus research from the post-Bultmannian perspective and attempts to demonstrate that the kerygma was implied in Jesus' words and deeds. Later Conzelmann announced that he was in agreement with Bultmann's position expressed in "The Primitive Christian Kerygma and the Historical Jesus" and would take no further part in the post-Bultmannian debate.

ROBINSON, JAMES M. *A New Quest of the Historical Jesus* ("Studies in Biblical Theology," No. 25). London: SCM Press, 1959. Robinson reviews the development of a "new quest" and sets forth a procedure to follow in the quest.

JEREMIAS, JOACHIM. "Der gegenwärtige Stand der Debatte um das Problem des historische Jesus." Wissenschaftliche Zeitschrift der Ernst Moritz Arndt-Universität Greifswald. Gessellschafts-und sprachwissenschaftliche Reihe 6 (1956–57), pp. 165–70. Published in English as "The Present Position in the Controversy Concerning the Problem of the Historical Jesus," *The Expository Times*, 69 (1958), 333–39. A later version of this essay was published as *Das Problem des historischen Jesus*.

Stuttgart: Calwer Verlag, 1960. Translated into English by NORMAN PERRIN as *The Problem of the Historical Jesus* ("Facet Books–Biblical Series," No. 13). Philadelphia: Fortress, 1964. In this essay Jeremias presents the current quest from a non-Bultmannian perspective.

BULTMANN, RUDOLF. *Das Verhältnis der urchristliches Christusbotschaft zum historischen Jesus.* Heidelberg: Carl Winter, Universitätsverlag, 1961. Translated into English by CARL E. BRAATEN and ROY A. HARRISVILLE as "The Primitive Christian Kerygma and the Historical Jesus," /*The Historical Jesus and the Kerygmatic Christ: Essays on the New Quest of the Historical Jesus.* New York: Abingdon Press, 1964, pp. 15–42. This is the address delivered in 1959 which gives Bultmann's reflections on the new quest.

CARLSTON, CHARLES EDWIN. "A *Positive* Criterion of Authenticity?" *Biblical Research,* 7 (1962), 33–44. Carlston sets forth a criterion to establish the authenticity of Jesus' sayings which compensates for Bultmann's negative criteria.

FULLER, REGINALD H. *Interpreting the Miracles.* Philadelphia: Westminster Press, 1963. A form critical approach to the miracles.

————. *The Foundations of New Testament Christology.* New York: Charles Scribner's Sons, 1965. Fuller treats Jesus' self-understanding as seen in his words and works and shows how the church in successive environments (Palestinian Judaism, Hellenistic Judaism, and the Graeco-Roman world) responded to Jesus by formulating a Christology. He applies the form critical method to the Synoptic tradition to distinguish between the materials from the earthly Jesus and those from the various periods of church activity.

McARTHUR, HARVEY K. "A Survey of Recent Gospel Research," *Interpretation,* 18 (1964), 39–55. Discusses four possible criteria of authenticity for the teaching of Jesus.

PERRIN, NORMAN. *Rediscovering the Teaching of Jesus.* New York: Harper and Row, 1967. A full-scale treatment of Jesus' teaching using form critical principles developed in line with the new quest.